What People Are ⋯ ⋯ bles

"To know Rosie is an ⋯ ⋯ ⋯or and connect with individuals ⋯ ⋯ from others. She has an innate ability to ⋯are in others' raw emotions, whether it be joyous celebrations or life-shattering turmoil. She has a gift of holding space for those who come across her path. She is a gift! With her plethora of life experiences, it has molded her into the strong, brave, and beautiful soul that she is. Being in her presence, whether in person or written form, you can't help but be washed over with comfort and peace."

—**Renée Avery**
Elementary School Teacher

"I have had the fortune and grace to have been on a part of Rosie's journey. Upon meeting at work, we became fast friends and have been colleagues and friends for over 16 years. Rosie presided over the marriage to the love of my life and was also the one to lay him to rest. We have been through thick and thin together; her soul-quenching love, determination and spiritual fortitude have seen and carried me and so many others through life's challenges. I am so grateful to still be a part of her amazing life; mine has been so enriched by her."

—**Annette Olson, M.A.**
Nonprofit Consultant

"I met Rosie in the late 1970s. Our lives and paths crossed many times through the 80s and 90s. It was during the time that I spent as a prison chaplain that I got to know and experience her deep faith and sense of compassion. I participated in several retreat and reflection days that she led for the chaplains. It was from these experiences that I invited Rosie to accompany an inmate who was facing the death penalty. I knew Rosie was the right person to accompany him on this journey. She embraced this invitation reluctantly at first and eventually wholeheartedly, as she has all of her ministries. We have been friends for many years and have shared much life. I am privileged to call her friend and celebrate the path her life and journey has taken her."

—**Michael Miriam Griego**
Retired Senior Manager
Material Management
The Boeing Company

Memories of My Life: Reflections of a Former Nun Led by the Spirit

ROSALIE G. ROBLES

Memories of My Life: Reflections of a Former Nun Led by the Spirit

For information about this title or to order other books and/or electronic media, contact the publisher:

Two Sisters Writing & Publishing®
TwoSistersWriting.com
18530 Mack Avenue, Suite 166
Grosse Pointe Farms, MI 48236

Hardcover: ISBN-13: 978-1-956879-60-5
Paperback ISBN: 978-1-956879-61-2
Ebook: ISBN: 978-1-956879-62-9

Printed in the United States of America
All the stories in this work are true.
Cover and Interior Design: Illumination Graphics.
Photos: The Robles Family Collection.
Cover photo: Jim Wolf.

This Book is dedicated to my
Dad and Mom.
Their belief in me and my
journey through life
was what sustained me!

Acknowledgements

This book has my name on it, but it is really the compilation of many people and circumstances that made this happen. I am eternally grateful for the intervention of the Holy Spirit that guided my steps through the many years of my ministry and throughout my life.

I am thankful to Cambridge Who's Who and Ashford Radio in New York, for initiating the circumstances that prompted me to tell my story.

To my Dad, for encouraging me to write this book.

And to my Mom, for telling me I could do this and to go for it!

To my husband Ron and sisters, Pat and Jooj, for being my cheerleaders throughout.

To my friend Joanie Lindenmeyer, for hearing of my dream and introducing me to Elizabeth Ann Atkins and her sister Catherine Greenspan of Two Sisters Writing & Publishing®. Thank you, Elizabeth, for editing my book and giving me invaluable help in making it make sense.

To Deborah Perdue of Illumination Graphics, for collaborating with me to design the cover and interior layout of this book.

To Jim Wolf, for taking the cover photo of me many years ago.

To Renee, Annette, and Michael, who all wrote such glowing endorsements, I hardly recognize myself!

To Cheech, who took time off from his incredible schedule to write the forward for me. Our life together is a book in itself!

To the Sisters in my former Community, especially Mary Margaret and Suzanne, who were happily surprised that I was actually writing this book and began to spread the news to the community.

To anyone whom I mentioned in the book, I thank you!

To all who came to my book launch and helped prepare for the event: Beth, Katie, Amy, Joanie, and Michael.

For all who have been a part of this incredible journey. Your presence gave me strength to move forward during difficult times and to celebrate accomplishments.

For my faithful companion Jake, my two-year-old pup who would come into my office during my creative moments and offer me a "lick" of support.

For my friends in my Valley and on Facebook, who showed such excitement and encouragement when they heard about the book.

And to so many more.

So, you see my name, but a host of family, friends, collaborators, and supporters is also here beside me.

My gratitude is boundless. This was truly a humbling experience.

Foreword by Cheech Marin

Lollie

Rosie . . . we called her Lollie.

Lollie and I are first cousins. Our mothers, Elsa and Ophelia, were sisters. We were raised in a large, tight-knit, blue collar, Chicano family in South Central Los Angeles. Our fathers were upholsterers, railroad workers, policemen, and everything in between. Our aunts and uncles had all gone to school together, and eventually they married and raised our large families in the same neighborhoods that they had been raised in.

The one other thing that we all had in common was that we were all Catholic, and—more importantly—that we all went to Catholic school. Parochial school for us was a classic liberal arts education that prepared us for college, which, unlike our parents, we were sure we were going to attend . . . unless something else intervened. That something else could be, for instance . . . a miraculous call to a vocation. In other words, becoming a priest or a nun.

It would be hard to escape the message, since it was broadcast all day, every day, and twice on Sunday.

"Pray for a vocation." It was intoned like a recruiting ad for the Marines. "There could be no higher calling . . ."

And we were all young and full of fervor. So eventually off we all went . . .

All the boys went to junior seminaries, all the boys . . . except me.

I was accepted to the Vincentian Jr. Seminary. My clothes had all been packed and sent to the school weeks before, and then that summer . . . I discovered girls. Soooo, that didn't work out.

But our one girl, the only female member of our inner sanctum of future "Holy Orders," would go on to have a full career as a nun, serving a community that you had to paddle to on a raft. Or was it a kayak? Anyway, you get the picture.

A girl, yes, but a girl who grew up with me as "one of the guys." Even as a small child, Rosie refused to change out of her OshKosh B'gosh overalls to put on a frilly dress with a bow in her hair when our family had company.

She also got into a lot of "trouble" because of our hijinks, especially with Rosie's brother, Louie, the revered instigator of mischief and adventure. The three of us were always together having fun, which we will always remember.

So who did this mischievous girl become as a grown woman?

Find out what happened next and learn what service really means.

I've known Lollie all my life. You are in good hands. So I encourage you to read this book and get to know what a multifaceted powerhouse she really is.

—Cheech Marin

Contents

Introduction

On these pages, you will read how the Holy Spirit repeatedly intervened in my life, moving me from event to event. This had convinced me that things do not happen by chance; even though we often do not recognize it at the time, we can see in retrospect how life's twists and turns have actually been orchestrated for our own good. However, we play a big part in this orchestration. We have to cooperate somehow as it unfolds.

A friend once told me, "Rosie, you live a charmed life." I had no idea what she meant at the time. I only knew that life was not routine for me. Things happened to me, and people came into my life without warning and changed me in some way. Some changes were for good, and some offered a challenge.

I will share with you stories and real-life situations that illustrate what I mean. It is amazing that all of these events could have happened in one single lifetime. They have taught me to trust the promptings of the Spirit. I sometimes follow these promptings, kicking and screaming and, at other times, willingly.

In 2010, Cambridge Who's Who, a publisher based in New York, called me and asked if they could feature me in their rather large volume of *Distinguished Professionals*. I had no idea what that meant, but I agreed to an interview.

They asked questions, and I answered the best I could. I had a working website at the time that described my ministry and some of my background, and they had gleaned some information from that ahead of time. Several plaques and commendations later, I was featured in the 2011 calendar of *Distinguished Professionals.* I was Ms. September.

The following year, Ashford Radio Station in New York saw the Cambridge write-up, and one of their producers asked if I would consent to a thirty-minute interview, broadcast live over the radio.

"Just share your life," the producer said.

In thirty minutes? I have lived several lifetimes in one, which was a challenge of its own, but describing them all in that short of time was another challenge altogether. Still, I wrote up my remarks to help me stay within the allotted time. Then I did the live radio interview by phone. After I hung up, the producer called back and said I had received a ninety-four percent rating from the listening audience. This success inspired them to invite me back for five more interviews.

"Just expound on the topics you touched on in the first interview," the producer said.

These interviews formed the basis of this book. My dad read each one several times and said, "Mija, did you really do all this?"

"I did, Pop."

"You should put these in a book."

A prompting of the Holy Spirit at work.

My life, as I have shared, has truly been a series of

undeniable steps in faith, which all required me to trust that there was a reason for each encounter or event. Today, looking back on over 57 years of direct ministry, I can see how, in some instances, God saved me from myself and, in others, how through prayer, I moved peacefully from one situation to another. Some life-altering, and all true.

This is my life—how the Spirit has led me, and miraculously how I have responded.

That's why I'm calling it *Memories of My Life: Reflections of a Former Nun, led by the Spirit.*

—Rosalie G. Robles

Chapter One

And so it begins . .

"I, Rosalie Robles, take you, Ronald Allen, to be my husband."

Wait, hold on a minute! People exclaimed.

What? You're Sister Rosie, this can't be!

And yet, it was!

This was a jolt for a lot of people who had known me for 35 years as Sister Rosie. They wondered, *who is this guy? He better be good to you, or he'll have to answer to us!*

It was hard for people to realize that before there was a Sister Rosie, there was a Rosie. And then Sister Rosie and Rosie again!

As I mentioned in the introduction, Ashford Radio Station in New York had invited me in 2012 to be interviewed by them live on air, during which they had asked me to "Just talk about your life." Well, okay, but how do you squeeze what, at the time, had been over 60 years' worth of lived experiences into a time slot of just thirty minutes?

Ah, the beauty of the written word. It knows no boundaries. Thinking I was going to get only one shot at this, I crammed in as much information as I could, by only grazing over my life to hit the high points. But now I realize that my life was worth much more than thirty minutes, and I have a lot more to say. So here goes!

I was born and raised in Los Angeles, California, as the second child of four. My brother, Louis, was a year older than me and my partner in crime. Then, along came my sister, Pat, and my youngest sister, Sylvia, whom we called Jooj.

My nickname was Lollie, as my brother couldn't pronounce Rosalie. To this day, my cousins don't know my given name. My parents, who are gone now, were my greatest supporters and always encouraged me to reach beyond their grasp. I was told that I could accomplish anything I put my mind to. My dad graduated from Woodbury College, now a university, with a degree in interior design and business. My parents were self-employed, proud owners of Robles Custom Furniture. I intuited their work ethic at a young age, having received an excellent Catholic education from elementary through high school.

I first had a desire to give my life to God when I was in grammar school. I think being taught by the good sisters instilled that desire in me at an early age. I didn't know much about anything, I admit. I observed the sisters during recess, and sometimes my parents would drive them to appointments, as nuns didn't drive then, and I would go along. Sometimes after school, I hung out at the convent for short periods of time. I even got invited inside, and believe me, I checked it out! The sisters were fun and kind and always looked happy. I loved the habit they wore, and I would try to fashion one for me to wear for Halloween. At home, I walked around the kitchen with an apron on my head to simulate their veil. It was no secret that this was what I wanted to be.

I went to an all-girls Catholic high school, Bishop Conaty Memorial. My brother went to an all-boys high school. We interacted between schools for events like dances, proms, and glee club performances. There was a huge event that all schools in the area participated in—kind of a talent show or jamboree that included Mount Carmel (my brother's school), Loyola (another boy's school), and St. Mary's Academy (a rival girls' school that my sisters eventually attended!). It was a big deal. My brother was a year older than me, so his friends were good dance partners.

We would sometimes host parties at our home. We would clear out the garage and decorate, and we would pick our favorite music to play on our small portable record player. I would invite my friends, and my brother would invite his. Mom and Dad hung around to enjoy the fun. They were loved and respected by our friends and were just a part of the crowd. Even then, I knew they were looking out for us.

I loved my high school years. We were taught by nine different communities of sisters. Sister Mary Carol was a Sister of Mercy and a mentor to me. I was young, and she didn't mind me hanging around and asking silly questions. We are friends to this day. Funny that I didn't enter her community.

I was committed to the Sisters of St. Joseph in my heart.

I didn't really date until my junior year. I was going to be a sister, after all. Then my cousin Margie asked me to be in her wedding. That's when I met John and Tony, who were groomsmen. Well, the convent began to fade away. Tony really liked me, but I really liked John! I went out with Tony a few times, but there was no spark, even though he was fun and made me laugh. John was several years older than Tony, and more mature.

Sister Rosalie was history! One day, John informed me that his job was relocating him out of state. What? My heart was broken. This was during my senior year, and there was no way I was going to go with him.

For our goodbye date, we went to the Pike, which was a huge amusement park, with carousels and Ferris wheels, and games and rides galore. When we were at the top of a double Ferris wheel, I gave him my graduation picture and said, "I'm going to enter the convent."

The look on his face was, well . . . shock!

"I've always wanted to do this," I said. Since he was moving, it felt like the perfect time to try it out . . . just in case.

He started rocking our chair to freak me out, as I do not like heights. That kind of broke the ice. He made me promise that if I didn't like it, I could come home, and we could reconnect. Well, I "tried it out" for more than 35 years!

Chapter Two

Rosalie Robles will be known in Religion as . . .

I entered the Sisters of St. Joseph of Carondelet in Los Angeles on September 8, 1963, right out of high school. I had given it what I thought was some serious consideration and prayer. This was IT . . . this was going to be the fulfillment of a dream.

John was gone (though we had talked for hours on the phone before I left), and I was free to pursue this step. My parents and grandparents, especially my grandmother, weren't too keen on the idea, but they didn't stand in my way. We were called Postulants as early recruits. I was going to make my mark in the world.

I got so homesick that I was literally physically ill. The rules and practices were foreign to me, but if this was what it took to fulfill my dream, then I would do it. I got in trouble often for breaking silence, or for causing the girls around me to break silence by joking around with them. We had a period of recreation where we could talk all we wanted, but not when silence was enforced. I am quick-witted, and when something strikes me, I just have to make a comment . . . not good!

Our motherhouse and college were situated in the hills of LA, in the Brentwood area. And as a result, we had to walk up a strenuous winding road just to get to class. My classmates, or Reception as we were called, put in some steps made from cut logs, so that we could take a shortcut up an embankment to get to class instead, which saved us the trouble of the more difficult journey up the road. In order for the embankment to not erode when it rained, we planted flowers of various kinds, especially ice plants, to hold the dirt in place. We called it "Penitential Hill" because whenever we got in trouble, we had to plant more flowers there for a period of time. I think they should have named that hill after me, as I planted a lot of flowers. I rarely had an internal thought that didn't come out my mouth!

I grew up in a family that enjoyed humor. We are all funny. I mean, my cousin Cheech—famous for being one half of the comedic duo Cheech and Chong—grew up with us. Since our mothers were sisters, Cheech was often with me and my brother Louie; we were one and two years apart in age. We all learned to be funny from my dad, who had a great sense of humor. It all came naturally to us. But convent living did not take kindly to my humor. I was eventually forced to adopt what they called "Religious Decorum!"

I started my freshman year at Mount Saint Mary's College, now a university. It was staffed and run by my community, and my Reception took college classes together. These were regular secular classes, like those that most freshmen took. After the first year, those of us who stayed received the holy habit and a new name. It was an exciting time. We made our habits from scratch. Nine yards of French Serge. The habit was fitted to us precisely. I still have the sewing box and scissors that my mom got for me. They are still as sharp as ever.

The ceremony to receive the habit was a highlight of my life. We were dressed in bridal gowns with a veil draped over our faces. I wore the prom dress that Mom made me and only removed the blue cummerbund around the waist. I wore it with white elbow-length gloves.

We processed in single file into the chapel. Our families were present, along with the families of the novices who were going to pronounce their temporary vows. The archbishop was also present. On the Communion rail was a black bundle that was our habit. After prayers and words from the archbishop, those of us who were going to receive the habit were dismissed. We filed out to music and the choir singing.

I had asked two sisters who were close to me, Sister Rose Anthony and Sister Joseph Adele, to dress me, as I had no clue how it all went on. They took my habit from the rail and met up with me in my alcove (dorm). I was instructed to have both the veil and my gloves taken off by the time I got to them. They removed my wedding dress and put the habit on me. One put my shoes on, while the other cut my hair and put on the headgear and veil. Believe me, it was quite involved and a lot for me to wear. Once dressed, we went into the hall and stood on a marker on the floor with our eyes cast down. We were not to look around to see how everyone looked. We were now in twos with our arms in our ample sleeves.

We proceeded to the doors of the chapel, waiting for our turn to reenter. Once the novices completed their vows, the doors opened, and the music and choir sang "The Contate." We had heard the choir practicing it for weeks, and now it was for real! My heart was beating to the rhythm of the hymn.

There was a subtle gasp from the people in the pews as they looked for and found their daughters, now in full habit. We were not to look around, but to approach the altar rail and kneel, because we were to receive our religious names. We could submit three choices. I submitted Raymond Carol, Louis Anthony, and Patricia Annette. We didn't know until this moment, as we knelt at the altar rail, what name we would receive. Finally, I heard, "Rosalie Robles will be known in religion as Sister Patricia Annette." My sisters' names, as Jooj's middle name was Annette. Tears filled my eyes. I was so happy, and I was finally a real sister. My best friend Antonia Roman entered with me, and she became Sister Carmen Anthony.

Later, at the luncheon with our families, we were able to hug and congratulate each other. It was fun locating everyone to see how they looked in the habit. We had to learn to pick up the front while walking upstairs and to hold the back while going down. Going up was the trick. I tripped many times, as I would rush up the stairs without thinking. Another dilemma was keeping our hair from sneaking out the side of the white cloth that surrounded our faces. Finally, we discovered that we could tuck the hair back in by using a fingernail file.

The habit was beautiful with its shear black veil. I wore it proudly and with honor.

Chapter Three

Prayer, study, classes, recreation,
meals, personal time, bed.

I became a novice, and that whole first year, we studied only Theology, the Bible as Literature, Christology, and History of the Congregation. We were taught by Dominican priests. Sister Laurentia taught History of the Congregation. We were "canonical" and immersed in non-secular studies.

Internally, things changed for me. I was Sister Patricia Annette. Every morning, I woke and dressed in the habit that I had so admired growing up. I felt different. I looked different. On visiting Sundays (that were once a month), my family knew I was different. We visited in the large parlor, or outside on the sundecks. There were groups of families in the parlor area, so we became friends with other families. I was the only one who could go beyond the frosted glass doors to our living and dining quarters.

Oftentimes, families would bring candy or food to share, and when visiting was over, we would bring the goods to the utility room and put them on the table. These would be parceled out little by little throughout the weeks. We would find a treat on our desks in the large study room, where we each had a desk in which we kept our books and personal items. We would study during the evening or when there was free time.

My parents got to know other parents. Several times during the year, there would be a work party for things that needed to be done around the grounds. Our dads would come to help out, so we got to sneak in an extra visit. Once the first year was completed and I was a second-year novice, I resumed regular sophomore classes.

One day, there was a notice on the board in the study room. Our novice director wanted us to come in and tell her our weight! Uh oh! Here we go, diets for everyone over the limit. Now, we always believed that lying was a sin, right? I can tell you that many of us fudged the truth! Nothing happened for a few days. One evening, as we were at recreation, we noticed that the blinds to the Novitiate (study room) were drawn.

"What's going on?" we wondered.

The bell rang, and we filed into the chapel for night prayers. When we got back to the Novitiate for an hour of study, there on each of our desks was a bathing suit!

"What in the world!!" we exclaimed.

We hadn't been swimming since we left home. I mean, it wasn't part of our lifestyle. However, at St. Martin of Tours Church, down the road, there was a swimming pool on the grounds. The home had once been owned by the movie star Gary Cooper. He had willed the property to the Church.

Our novice directors thought it would be a treat for us to be able to use the pool occasionally. Thus, the swimsuits. We were asked to put them on, and one of the directors would come around and check to see that they were modest enough. You could hear them laughing down the hall as they checked out the suits. It was a sweet idea, but awkward. Especially on the day that we actually did go swimming. Some couldn't swim, and some were diving off the board! I can't remember if we had to take off the habit or wear it down to the pool under our bathrobe. I just recall many of us clinging to the side of the pool while the novice directors sat in lounge chairs, egging us on. If your suit didn't fit, it was because you lied!

On some Saturdays during recreation, we would mingle with the postulants for folk dancing or a walk off the grounds to the bridge, which was just down the hill and around the neighborhood. That was enjoyable, and it was a way for us to get to know the new group of girls who had entered that year.

Our life was simple: prayer, study, classes, recreation, meals, personal time, and bed. Lights out at ten and up at five. We were being prepared for an eventual mission experience. All in all, we were happy. However, it was not uncommon for someone to decide that this wasn't the life for them, and with guidance from the postulant or novice directors, they would decide to leave. We never knew who had left until we saw their name on the blackboard in the study room. We were cautioned not to discuss it. That was hard on all of us, as we had become friends with one another, and losing someone was losing a friend.

My friend Antonia left as a first-year novice. I was called into the novice director's office, and she informed me that Antonia had gone home. The director knew that we had been friends since childhood, so she gave me that courtesy. I didn't see her again for several years. Then, one day, she came to visit me when I was teaching in Redondo Beach. Then, many years later, I called her to inform her that a sister she was close to had died in a car accident. After that call, we never communicated again. I don't know why!

Years later, my graduating class from high school was having our fiftieth reunion, and one of the gals who was coordinating it contacted me, because she was trying to locate members of our class. She couldn't find Tonia (Antonia). I knew her birth date and gave it to Donna Miller, as she had access to locating people from an internet application. A few hours later, she called me and informed me that Tonia had died several years earlier. She gave me her sister Mary's phone number so I could call and reacquaint with her and find out about Tonia's life and final days. That made me wish I had taken the time to find her over the years. To this day, I miss her, as we were best friends for many years.

Several young women went home during the first three years. I often wonder where they are and how they are doing. I am glad to have reconnected with several women on Facebook who were part of those formative years with me.

Chapter Four

OBEDIENCE is one of our vows.

I made my temporary vows the following year and became a junior professed sister. We moved to the other side of the motherhouse, and each of us had our own room with our own bathroom. No more dorm. No more standing in line, in silence, waiting for a shower to be free. A dresser, a desk, a closet, and a bed. I loved my privacy. It seemed like our personal time was more frequent. There was a small kitchen for us to use when we came down the hill after class, where we could grab a quick lunch if we had missed the formal gathering.

Being a young, professed sister, I received a beautiful crucifix that hung around my neck, just under the cape or large white celluloid collar that was part of the habit. We were free to interact with the older junior professed sisters who were a year ahead of us. Our time was much more relaxed. The Reception ahead of us was going to be sent out, or missioned, at the end of the year, to a school where they would teach, or to have an experience in a hospital setting. In those days, we only had two choices as to what our field of emphasis would be: either teaching or healthcare. I knew nursing was not my thing, so teaching it was!

Meanwhile, my major had been changed several times. I wanted to be an art major. I was told that a Spanish major and education minor were more suited to the needs of the community, since I was so far away from graduation and the community needed four of us to teach during the upcoming school year. As a result, I was pulled from my college classes and given a crash course on how to teach second grade. So, for two weeks, a professed sister educated us on classroom protocol while we made color charts for our classroom. I was assigned to St. James School in Redondo Beach, California.

I lived in a house with twelve sisters during the week and went to class at our college on the weekends. On my first day in the classroom, I was at my desk in full habit. I was twenty-two years old, and a little boy named Kieran came in to greet me. He had a stammer, and he said, "Wuuh, wuuh are you our teacher?"

"I am," I said, trying to sound adult and calm.

He looked at me with large blue eyes and said, "Wuuh, wuuh, I guess you're buu-buu-better than nothing."

And so, it began! I loved my class and especially Kieran. I remained at St. James for three years.

While there, I learned how to play the guitar. Sister Timothy Joseph taught me. She was a good friend with a great sense of humor. Also, Vatican II was in full swing, and a lot of changes took place. I changed from the traditional habit to a more contemporary dress with a small veil that allowed my hair to show. I was given the option of returning to my given name. So, over the Christmas vacation, I made all those changes. I told my class that they were going to have a new teacher when they came back from Christmas break. When the bell rang for us to line up outside, there I was. Sister Rosalie in a dress that revealed my legs and a veil that showed my hair. Needless to say, I had their full attention for some time.

The summer before my last year at St. James, I underwent emergency back surgery. I entered the hospital after school was out in June, and I stayed until the end of August. It was a delicate surgery that put me in a steel brace from my shoulders to my hips for six months. Immediately after surgery, as they were transferring me back to my room, I vaguely recall a nurse saying rather urgently to take me back up to surgery, as I had developed a blood clot and was having difficulty breathing.

I opened my eyes slightly, enough to see my parents and my dad leaning over me with tears in his eyes. I closed my eyes, and everything became black except for a bright light in the distance. That's all I saw. When I woke up, I was told that when they got me back in surgery, the blood clot was gone. Was that a sign that God had plans for me? By October, I was back in the classroom with a brace. My mom made shift-type dresses to go over the brace. Barely able to walk, I had a rough time teaching second graders. The sisters were helpful to me. I managed.

I remember one day, while with a reading group, I sat on a small chair while they were sitting on carpet samples in front of me. A boy reached out and touched my leg. Embarrassed, he tried to apologize. I knew he was fascinated that I had legs. I reached over, tasseled his hair, and smiled at him. He put his head down and wouldn't look at me for the rest of our reading session. It took a while before they got used to the new me. It took me a while, too!

My mom was an accomplished seamstress. She made quite a few outfits out of the black serge that our habits were made from.

Toward the end of the school year, I was approached by a sister in administration. She was visiting each community to see how we were all doing. She met with each of us individually. I was on schedule to make my final vows in a few years, so she said it was important that I have another mission experience before I took those vows.

"Do you have any requests for transfer?" she asked. "Any place you would like to go?"

Wow, I remember thinking, *they never ask us our opinion of things like this.*

So, I said, "I would like to stay in the Los Angeles area, as my family is there. And if possible, teach middle grades." Since I knew that Prescott, Arizona was open, I said, "And not a place starting with a P."

Obedience is one of the vows we take when we are received into the community as either a temporary or a finally professed sister, along with the vows of Poverty and Chastity. We spend long hours studying what each of them means. Poverty: We don't own anything in our name. Any paycheck we get for our ministry goes to the greater community. We will be cared for for the rest of our lives, but we will be dependent on the community for our livelihood. Chastity: Well, we are now Brides of Christ, so marriage is out of the question. Okay, I kind of get how those two work. Obedience was altogether different. You don't question. You do as you're told.

Well, I knew I was going to be transferred, so I was eagerly awaiting the list to see where I was off to. So, the list came out, and there was my name. It said Sister Rosalie is missioned to St. Patrick's school in Pasco, Washington, to teach first grade. Yes, whatever you are thinking or saying . . . were my thoughts and words exactly!!

Chapter Five

The Spirit is moving all over this land . . .

The school year ended, and by the end of the summer, I was off to Pasco, Washington to teach at St. Patrick's school. I had never been out of California, so I would make this an adventure. I was in a house with six other sisters. We were all busy getting our classrooms ready for the first day.

I loved setting up my room. I had several stations. The students were in groups named after colors, and they moved from station to station while a group was with me for reading. They could go to "Workshop," where I had set up several games that I had made to help them develop skills. In the "Rock and Read" corner, I had arranged small rocking chairs that they had brought in from home (if they had one), where they could sit and read any of the books in a library setting. Easy books, mostly pictures, with only a few words. They were learning to read. There was a stack of carpet samples that they could sit on while in the reading group with me. There was "Seat Work," where they could pull a mimeographed paper from a file with math problems on it.

My classroom was bright with primary colors, on the small folding chairs I had spray painted, as well as on a low table where they could do their seat work rather than at their desks. I was going to enjoy these little guys. However . . . A week before school started, our Spanish teacher quit for personal reasons. Our school went up to the ninth grade, since the high school began at grade ten, and it was required that we offer a year of a foreign language before they went on to high school. There was no longer a teacher available to do it, so I was asked to take that on. Sister Diane would teach science to my class while I instead taught ninth-grade Spanish. Why me? Because I was both a Spanish major and Hispanic. Oh, and obedience played a part in this decision. My major had been changed to Spanish just before I left for Pasco. I had never even taken Spanish One, and I was put in Linguistics and Advanced Conversation when I studied during the summer. Seriously! I'm not kidding!

Teaching the ninth grade began as a challenge. Especially after lunch, when everyone was sleepy and their behavior was a far cry from my little people, discipline-wise. I was twenty-five years old, and the students knew I was young and barely knew what I was doing.

I would memorize the dialogue at the beginning of each chapter, and because I had good pronunciation thanks to having listened to my parents speaking Spanish to their parents, I sounded credible. Seat of your pants teaching! I found a way to make it fun for me too. One year, we made pinatas, maracas, and an awesome Mexican dinner for the staff.

I moved up to fourth grade after three years and was able to teach my "firsties" again as fourth graders. It was a great year. I used my guitar a lot when I taught. This fourth-grade class was very musical. We put on an Up With People production for the school and the parents. Up with People is a nonprofit organization that promotes positive thinking and racial equality through song and dance. With instruments, stage props, and 12 songs to sing, our performance was magical! Every three songs, everyone on stage would move to a different spot. The choreography was perfect.

We were invited to perform at St. Joseph's school in a neighboring town. They assembled their student body in the auditorium, and we did our thing. In the middle of one of the songs, my guitar string broke. Everyone stopped singing for a moment and stared at me. I waved my hand and told them to keep singing. With a pounding heart, I took a deep breath and sang along with them while I restrung the D string, tuned up again, and continued the song. My kids didn't let me down.

While at St. Pat's, I got close to several students in the older grades. I offered to teach guitar to those who wanted to learn. I had a friend in Manhattan Beach who ran a music studio and sold guitars. We became good friends. I drew his portrait, and he taught me a lot about chords and how to care for a guitar. He gave me a new Alvarez classical guitar when I made my final vows.

Many sisters were able to get a deal at Gene Leis Studio. He put a deal together called the "Sister Rosalie Special": a classical guitar, strap, capo, guitar case, pitch pipe, extra set of strings, and a sidewinder to help wind the strings. All for a whopping 39 dollars. I sold a lot of those guitars for my students who wanted to learn. Garret Freight would pull into the schoolyard, unload several guitars at a time, and repeat it as more guitars were ordered.

At one time, over those years, I had as many as 52 students. I grouped them, and we would play for the 10 AM Mass on Sunday. I loved it. I was in my element and was perfecting my guitar skills as well. I even had a group of parents who wanted to learn the guitar. They called themselves "The Over the Hill Group."

Those years at St. Pat's were filled with personal growth. I became involved in Holy Spirit spirituality. The Charismatic Renewal was a new phenomenon. I wanted to learn more.

One summer, my friend Sister Mary Margaret and I made our eight-day retreat at a retreat center in Palos Verdes, California. The priest conducting the retreat was filled with the Holy Spirit in a tangible way. He invited any of us who wanted to attend a prayer meeting at Loyola University. I signed us up in a car, and off we went to a prayer meeting like I had never attended before. A cordial group, all sitting in a circle with a gentleman who introduced himself and welcomed us newcomers. The meeting started with a few songs.

Hands began to rise, and people were showing an exuberance I was unfamiliar with. People were talking to themselves in praise, and at one point, someone spoke out in the first person as if Jesus Himself was speaking. Another time, someone spoke in a language I did not understand. Someone across the room immediately interpreted what was said. My eyes were wide open. I had no idea.

Then, one person began to sing. Nothing I had ever heard before. No words, just a cadence. Those who knew how blended their own voices in, and the most beautiful sound arose to a loud crescendo and gradually died down. I could not join in; I could only listen. All I could think was, *this is what a choir of angels sounds like.*

Following the meeting, we all went over to the chapel on campus for Mass. After Mass, a priest said that several people would be available to pray with others. I moved up to the front pew and just sat. Mary came with me. Then I saw this priest standing on the steps in front of the altar, looking right at me. My index finger summoned him, and he came and sat beside me. Mary moved to the far end of the pew.

"I really don't know why I called you over," I told him.

"I was drawn to you in the front row for some reason," he said with a kind demeanor and gentle voice.

He took my hand and placed the other on my shoulder. Very quietly, he began to pray. He spoke specifically of my needs, but he couldn't have known what my needs were. I sat with my eyes closed while he spoke about my fears and my questions about my faith. A calm came over me, and I began to cry. Not a sob, just gentle tears filling my eyes. He left my side, and I never saw him again.

I became consumed with Scripture. It was as if the words were brand new and jumping off the pages, speaking just to me. Meanwhile, my friend said she kept her eyes on me and could see something had happened to me. My prayer became personal, and I spoke with a newfound belief. I was not afraid to proclaim my faith, but I did so quietly.

After this experience, I became involved with the Charismatic Renewal Movement. I joined a prayer group and invited some of my ninth graders to join me at a prayer meeting. It was a very spiritually fruitful time in my life. The Holy Spirit was unleashed in my ministry in a profound way. I had an inner happiness that I could never really describe, but people saw it in me.

Chapter Six

Off to the Inner City in Los Angeles

Itook a group of high school students to Immaculate Heart Retreat House in Spokane for a spirit-filled weekend run by skilled young adults. These young adults had invited me to be a part of their team for the weekend. I mostly just listened, but I had a chance to say a word or two. The teens were enthralled and filled with joy and gratitude when we were on our way home.

After that, I received a call from Monsignor who was the director and founder of the Retreat House, asking me if I had ever thought about doing full-time retreat work, specifically with youth. I had never given it much thought, especially since I was being groomed for teaching. I was young and didn't think I could ask my superiors to release me from teaching to work at a Retreat House instead. He said he was wanting to start a small community of laypeople, who would live in a house on the property and give Life In The Spirit Seminars at the Retreat House on given weekends.

I thought about the priest who prayed with me at Loyola U after Mass. He prayed that the Holy Spirit would become my strength and inspiration, and that God would lead me to where I could proclaim His word through the inspiration of the Spirit. Was this where I was being led?

I took a leap of faith and approached my community about the possibility of leaving teaching to work at the Retreat House at Monsignor's invitation. They didn't give me an answer right away. Finally, I was told that the community couldn't release me this year, that they wanted me to teach for one more year, but then we could see where things were after that and make a decision then. I shared their conclusion with Monsignor, and he agreed to wait a year. That would give him time to recruit other interested adults who would be willing to form a spirit-filled community.

Meanwhile, I continued to be involved in a prayer group in Pasco, and I attended meetings and prayer experiences in Spokane and neighboring cities. I was anxious for this new year to end, so I could find out where I would be sent for my final year of teaching and return to become a member of a spirit-filled community, who shared beliefs that openly displayed the gifts of the Spirit.

I left St. Patrick's with a heavy heart, as I had grown to love the students, and many of the families had taken to me as one of their own. My ninth-grade guitar students had graduated to Pasco High, but I still had many students who were eager to learn, and I hated to leave them. I knew I would be back in Eastern Washington in a year and could find a way to connect again.

I was sent to teach in the inner city of Los Angeles. I had seventh-grade homeroom, but I taught eighth-grade language arts as well. St. John Evangelist School was in a rough part of Los Angeles. The students were great, but very different from my Pasco kids. They were street-smart. Some had family members who were members of local gangs. Violence was part of the daily happenings in the city. My students nicknamed me "Sistah Love."

It was great being so close to my family again. I could go home on weekends and attend family celebrations. It had been years since I had been home for my own birth-day. I was amazed at how the younger cousins I had left behind when I entered the convent were now married and had children of their own.

At the time, my sister Jooj was dating an aspiring musician, Jim. He had written a beautiful song entitled "Saddening Surprise." He and his brother, Chuck, had worked on the lyrics and music with violins and a full orchestra. The music was recorded, and all they needed was someone to sing the song over the music. I was given that privilege. This was going to be a demo that would be taken to various record labels in the hopes that he could get a contract, as he had many other songs to share.

I am not a soprano, nor am I an alto. I am somewhere in between. This song was within my range until, at a certain point, I was supposed to reach a high note and hold it for a second. We tried over and over until my voice was hoarse. Then, I was an alto. I have no idea if it went anywhere, but I have a copy of it, minus the messed-up parts. I had a pass-able voice in those days!

I taught my sisters and my cousin, Monica, to play the guitar. We would meet every Monday evening in the con-vent. One night, we had just finished and were going to meet Pat's husband, George, for dinner at a nearby restau-rant. They were parked across the street in front of the convent. As we walked out, I noticed two guys standing at the corner under the streetlight.

"If anything happens," I told my sisters and my cousin, "run and scream!"

Sure enough, as we were putting the guitars in the trunk of the car, the two guys walked slowly as if to pass us and suddenly lunged at us. Jooj and Monica ran, scream-ing, and hid in the front yard of a house. Pat and I were right in their line of attack.

They grabbed our purses and hit me across my chest. I fell backward. They picked Pat up and threw her on top of me. No one came out to see what the noise was, but several called the police. By the time the police arrived, the guys were long gone. The police found our purses a few days later; no money, of course. I had two dollars folded up between two pictures. They never found them!

I had fallen hard and treated myself to a hot bath and some aspirin. This was in the early seventies. I didn't see a doctor; I just kept teaching. I was flanked by my eighth-grade boys like a protective shield. Wherever I went, they went with me. The people were angry that we were assaulted and vowed to find out who did this. I don't know if they did, but if so, you can bet they were dealt with.

It was hard for me to shake what had happened. I hated being in an elevator or doorway with a man alone. Everywhere I went, people walking toward me seemed like potential attackers. They could hurt me. Even to this day, I look around when I go into a store. I make it a point to make eye contact with anyone coming toward me, and I give them a big smile as if to say, "Hi, I'm a good person; please don't hurt me." I missed my bodyguards.

At the end of that year, I left for Spokane.

Chapter Seven

"Please Lord, not again!"

My teaching days were behind me, and I was beginning a new career as Retreat Director. I was not yet thirty and was working alongside some of the holiest men I would ever know: Bishop Bernard Topal, and Jesuit priests Father Armand Nigro and Father Vince Beuzer, my spiritual director. His gift of discernment was legendary.

Father Beuzer and Father Nigro were the founders of the Credo Program at Gonzaga University. The program involved a year of personal growth for both priests and sisters who were taking a sabbatical year off. I was privileged to conduct Faith Sharing Retreat weekends for participants in the program, and I was a spiritual director to a number of participants during the year.

During that time, I developed a prayer life that has stayed with me to this day. I studied the Spiritual Exercises of St. Ignatius, and I was guided by Fathers Nigro and Beuzer toward a Spiritual Director Certification. Looking back, I can see the hand of God preparing me for a ministry that would define me and give credibility to my eventual private practice. I was totally clueless about what was waiting for me around the corner.

I wasn't at the Retreat House for very long when I began to feel a familiar sensation in my lower back. I ignored it at first and didn't say anything to anyone, because I was finally doing what I thought God had intended for me. The discomfort lingered longer than I had wanted. I finally mentioned it, and I was immediately told to go to bed and rest for several days.

As long as I was lying down, the pain was tolerable. Until one day, I stood up and couldn't walk. I fell back onto the bed and told the next person who came in to check on me that I was in bad shape. Someone called 911, and an ambulance took me to Sacred Heart Hospital. I feared the worst, and while lying in an examining room, I prayed, "Dear Lord, not again, please!"

The doctor came in and confirmed my fear. My fusion was compromised.

"Have you fallen recently?" he asked. "In the last few years?"

I couldn't think of anything until he said the crack didn't look new and had filled in with scar tissue. It had become weak and was now pressing on the spinal column. I told him about the mugging a few years ago and how I had fallen hard on my back.

"That's what did it," he said. "We need to go in and repair it."

He assured me that it wouldn't be as involved as the initial surgery. My parents flew into Spokane for the surgery and stayed a few weeks. There was no way I could resume my responsibilities. I had brought the brace with me, and I would wear it when I had pain. My superiors said that I needed to leave to recuperate without feeling guilty for not working.

My good friend, Sister Mary Margaret, had taken a position as principal at a school in Lewiston, Idaho. She offered to come and take me to the convent there, so she could look after me until I was strong enough to return to the Retreat House.

"Oh, thank you, God," I exclaimed. "They're not sending me to Los Angeles." At least I had a good chance of continuing my training as Spiritual Director. I laid in the back seat of her car for the three-hour trek to Lewiston.

Now back in the brace and using a cane, I got around pretty well. One afternoon, as we were walking across the street to attend Mass, a lady stopped me and asked, "Are you Sister Rosalie from the Retreat House in Spokane?"

I felt glad that I wasn't forgotten.

She said, "We saw the article about you in the newspaper, quite by accident as we were lining our wastebasket, when we saw your smiling face."

Well, that was a gut punch right in the humility basket!

Mary asked me, "What did she say?"

"She saw my picture in the paper."

"Well, that was sweet of her to tell you."

"Yep, real sweet!"

Monsignor came to visit halfway through my convalescence. He assured me that they were anxious for my return. Whew! Such a relief!

Sitting put a lot of stress on my spine, so it was best for me to either stand or lie down. I learned to crochet. I made everyone a hat and scarf. We were in snow country, so why not? Right? I was loved and cared for by the sisters in the house. We were across the alley from the sisters who worked at the hospital, and many would come over to see how I was doing.

Eventually, I felt good enough to go back to the Retreat House. One of the priests who worked there had his pilot's license and offered to come and get me to fly me back to Spokane. He called and said, "I need to know how much you weigh."

Are you kidding me? I asked, "Why?"

I was wearing a steel brace that weighed a few pounds, plus I had my suitcase. He was bringing a visiting priest along with him and could only have so much weight aboard the plane, plus the gas. It was a four-seat, high-wing Cessna!

Mary drove me to the local country airport. We were standing behind a wire fence, waiting for Father Beno to arrive. There, in the distance, was this very small object that resembled a dragonfly. Mary said, "I think that's your plane!"

No way! There was no turning back. I had to do it. I gave Mary a hug and said, "Pray for me." I lumbered up the ladder-like steps and sat in the back with my suitcase. I looked at Mary, who looked apprehensive. She gave a weak smile as Father Beno turned the plane around to get ready for takeoff. We had to clear a huge, mountainous hill, the same hill that you descend when driving into town.

He revved the engine, and we started to pick up speed. The hill was coming closer, and we were still on the ground. I heard Father say, "Come on, baby, get up there."

I shut my eyes as we barely cleared the top and climbed higher. I do not like to fly, and this was a "never again" experience. I thought!

The visiting priest was happy, taking pictures out the small window. Every time he attempted to stand or move, the plane would swerve and had to be corrected. I sat with my eyes slammed shut! I thought, *please, God, no trick flying!*

As we approached Spokane, we began our descent.

"When we get low enough," Father Beno said over the engine noise, "I am going to shut off the engine, and we will glide to a landing."

I was sure this was the end of the line for me. He did, and we did. It was a bumpy landing, but we made it.

He called me "Rosie Baby," which I was not fond of, and asked, "How did you like that landing?"

I had no voice, and he could tell by the flushed look on my face that I would never fly with him again!

Chapter Eight

I tried not to look, but I couldn't avoid it.

While at the Retreat House, I worked towards perfecting my talks and preaching skills. I continued to offer Life in The Spirit Seminars. I worked with the youth in the area by offering them weekend retreat experiences. That is how I met Sister Lynda Bowen, a Franciscan Sister who was the Religious Education Coordinator at St. Peters Parish, just down the road from the Retreat House. Together, we worked as a team with the youth, and we remained a team for more than 15 years.

Many wonderful friendships blossomed while I studied and learned Ignatian Spirituality (Spiritual Exercises of St. Ignatius). I played my guitar at Mass and before every guest speaker.

During this time, I met the wonderfully talented Millie Reith. I had been playing and singing her songs for years at Mass and retreats. We became close friends. She was a short, slight woman with an amazing voice. We would sing and play together. We taped ourselves on a reel-to-reel recorder.

We would harmonize with each other and did voice-on-voice duets. I wrote several songs, including a complete Mass, and she helped me to put them to notated music. I do not read music, but she did, and she was a great help to me. Her music was played and sung for years all over the United States. The seventies were very fertile for "folk music," and guitar Masses were the norm. The Monks of Weston Priory and Saint Louis Jesuits, along with Millie Reith, were the go-to hymns.

As young as I was, I was learning, and my position at the Retreat House continued to afford me amazing experiences. For example, Monsignor and I conducted a week-long retreat for priests in British Columbia, Canada. I was treated kindly and received well by the men when I spoke and played my guitar. I was quite inexperienced, but I felt that I had a message to share, and they listened. I had a room on the other side of a door that opened up to the priests' quarters. The room was sparse, and the bed slanted downward, so I turned the bed around so I would roll against the wall at night instead of onto the floor.

They would play jokes on me, like flickering the lights off when I was in the shower upstairs in a vacant part of the Monastery. When our week was up, we had become friends. They apologized for the jokes, which made Monsignor a bit perturbed. I knew they were only teasing, as not many women graced their halls like I did.

I received a book before we left, titled *Hello Sunshine*. It was signed by all 26 priests. I had made an impression on them, especially one of them in particular, who wrote:

To Our Rosie,
Smile for me with your eyes!
People are like colors in a Rainbow.
The Rainbow is Our Lord Jesus!
Sharing your color, Rosie, with me
has enriched my color.
Ever searching, growing, and believing
what lies at the end of
Our Rainbow.

We are one in the Spirit (Rainbow)
So, I do not believe in goodbyes.
Smile with your color, Rosie
Thanks, I need that!

I never shared the book with Monsignor, as he would not have approved of their obvious fondness for me. In a way, he had begun to think of me as his private companion. This became uncomfortable for me as the year went on.

From there, we flew to the Provence of Alberta to give some talks to a community of sisters. I usually led with a few songs with my guitar. This time, I gave a talk on the Gifts of the Spirit. There was a young sister sitting in the front row, directly in front of me. After we finished, she asked to see me. As she questioned me, I found her a bit odd. She was a little jumpy. She said that she was a nurse, and that she found what I said interesting. Wearing a corduroy suit, she had blond hair cut short. She was slight in build. Her gaze throughout my talk was somewhat disturbing. I tried not to look at her, but I couldn't avoid it.

Meanwhile, I noticed that the good sisters made a fuss over Monsignor, making sure he had everything he needed and more. In contrast, I was left to carry my own suitcase and guitar. No fuss over me. Though, they were cordial enough. This was a far cry from the attention I had received with the priests just a few days earlier.

While flying home, Monsignor handed me a twenty-dollar Canadian bill, and thanked me for accompanying him.

Chapter Nine

Francis knew she was possessed.

My three years at the Retreat House were both enriching and challenging. Many well-known speakers came to offer seminars and/or retreat experiences. One well-known author and speaker stands out as one of the most incredible experiences of my life—Francis MacNutt, a former priest renowned in the Healing Ministry, who was a teacher, pioneer, and theologian. People were healed by his touch.

He came to offer a week on healing. Not just to anyone, but only to individuals who were in the healing profession: doctors, nurses, psychologists, and anyone who worked with people professionally for their well-being. I was excited to meet him, as I had read his first book, *The Power to Heal*. I felt called to the Healing Ministry for some reason.

Francis had arrived earlier and got settled in. I was honored to meet him and make him feel welcome. As participants began to arrive, I was at the main entrance, greeting and welcoming them. There, in the midst of the crowd, was the sister—the one with the odd stare—whom I had met in Alberta. She was a nurse, so she qualified for attendance. I did not have a good feeling about it.

Monsignor welcomed everyone, and I started the evening with my guitar and a few songs that I was hoping everyone knew. I was intentionally keeping my distance from the sister from Alberta. But there she was, front and center, while I played my guitar.

The participants were enthusiastic. I recognized many from our area and some who had made retreats there before. I felt at home and proud to be a member of the hosting Retreat House. Francis had us introduce ourselves as part of the staff. He said that we would be available if anyone wanted a private moment of prayer as the week went on. *Uh oh*, I thought, *this could be just the invitation she wanted to get to me.* Sure enough, before the night was over, she approached me and asked if I would be her spiritual director for the week.

I was not in a position to say no. We made an appointment where she would come to my office each day to share her prayer experience or thoughts after each of Francis's talks. She always showed up early—half an hour early! I would open the door when leaving my office, and she would already be sitting there. With no apologies, she would walk in and sit down and take her hour, plus extra. I finally had to be a bit stern with her and say, "We have to adhere to our agreed-upon time, as I have other people to see as well."

That didn't seem to matter, as she was always still there, outside my office, when I arrived. But instead of letting her into my office, I would smile and go up the stairs and not invite her in until her scheduled time. One day, at our appointed time, she shared with me that on her walk, she had come across the molted skin of a snake. She had it taped inside the pages of her journal. She was fascinated with snakes, she told me. Then, she lifted her pant leg and showed me her skin. It eerily resembled the skin of a snake.

I would find her in places where she had no business being, like in the boiler room. I had gone there to get something for the sisters in the kitchen, and there she was, just staring. I shared this when we met as a team each afternoon. Francis was concerned about how participants were taking his talks and if there were any problems we had encountered. I told him and the group about my discomfort with this particular person. He cautioned me to keep a friendly distance and to let him know if things escalated in any way. I was comforted knowing that he was looking out for me.

One evening, while I was in line for dinner, she frantically approached me. She needed to talk to me right then.

"I'm in line for dinner," I said. "It's not a good time."

She grabbed my arm, and I grabbed hers to remove her hands from me. She got the idea and left in a huff. Later that evening, she showed me that my hand had left a red mark on her arm. She wanted to know what kind of power I possessed. I was stumped!

Father Vince asked if he could come to my office after the evening conference. He wanted me to pray with him for the release of the Holy Spirit in a charismatic way. Francis was heavily involved in the Catholic Charismatic Renewal movement and referred to it often in his talks. Father Vince knew that I was also involved in the Renewal and had experienced firsthand the operative gifts of the Spirit. He wanted that in his ministry. Sister Lynda was at the retreat and knew Father Vince, so she joined us for prayer. Father Vince was a very humble priest. I mean, here I was, for all intents and purposes, a spiritual fledgling, and he was asking me to pray for him, a professor of theology. We prayed, and the Spirit overcame him. It was mystical and magical at the same time.

The next morning, when I went to breakfast, a lady came up to me and asked if I was aware of what had taken place last night in the chapel. I told her I was not aware of anything. Just then, a member of the staff came and said that Francis wanted to talk to me. I picked up my breakfast and went into the guest dining room, where Francis was seated. He invited me to sit down and apologized for inter-rupting my breakfast. He needed to bring me up to date on the happenings of last night.

Apparently, my retreatant had come to my door to talk to me and had heard voices inside, so she decided to go into the chapel to see if Francis was available. Each night, after the evening talk, he invited anyone who wanted to be prayed with to come into the chapel. He would be available for a blessing, and if more time were needed, he would arrange to see the person at a later time.

Francis' prayers were so powerful that many peo-ple were laying all over the floor of the chapel. The phenomenon was known as being "slain in the Spirit." He would lay hands on a person, and they would go down. It doesn't happen to everyone, but it did for many that night. When her turn came, Francis put his hands on her head, and she began to scream and flung herself down on the ground with grunts and howling sounds.

He recognized immediately that she was possessed by evil spirits. He took her, dragging her into the back sacristy, where the priest vests for Mass. He was accompanied by a few others who had traveled with him and understood what was going on. He asked those in the chapel to pray in the name of Jesus for her and for him. Scripture says, "in the name of Jesus, all evil must flee." This lasted for several hours. He was able to cast out the lesser evil spirits, but the big guns would need more time. He bound them so they could not hurt her, and he gave her the name of a priest in her vicinity who could help her.

She told him that her grandfather, Adolf, used to fool around with the occult in the basement of their house. She was only a child and would go down there and crawl around while he was invoking evil spirits. So she had become possessed at an early age.

As I said, she had struck me as having a confused state of mind when we had first met. Now, Francis told me that she wanted to see me. He said for me to walk around in front of the Retreat House where he could see me with her. He warned against getting into a discussion about last night. He doubted that she would bring it up, but just in case she did, he said, I should steer clear.

We met, and she was more subdued than I'd ever seen her. She was almost embarrassed. I never mentioned what had happened the night before. She wanted to know if it would be alright if she wrote to me, and if I would write her back. I told her that would be okay. She said that Francis had given her the name of a priest near her who would continue to help her. I encouraged her to follow through with his suggestion. She gave me a hug, and she left for home before the retreat was over. I heard from her a few times, and then all correspondence stopped.

Chapter Ten

Spiritual Direction Certification

*I*was moving at breakneck speed, spiritually. I needed time to process all I'd been through, so I asked for the opportunity to make a thirty-day silent retreat. If I were eventually going to direct people in that experience, it stood to reason that I should experience it myself. Besides, I needed some downtime. So I left my office and took a room down the hall, like any retreatant would.

Sister Miriam was my director for the month. She had been on the staff at the Retreat House for a number of years. She was quite a bit older than me and well-seasoned.

She asked me at one point if I had retired rather early. Here I was, being trained at an early age to do what she was doing in her late fifties. I think she was a little taken aback by this young, guitar-slinging sister on the staff. Since this was a silent retreat, the only time I spoke was during daily meetings with Sister Miriam in her office upstairs. As my spiritual director, she guided my prayer. I knew the ropes by then and was privy to any questions she might ask me.

I was on guard and ready to defend my aspirations at such a young age in comparison to her.

It took a while for me to settle down and allow her to lead me through the scripture and see how God was directing me. The experience itself turned out to be beneficial, and we both discovered a new respect for one another.

I was surrounded by holiness. Visiting priests would come in to be a part of the team directing retreats that lasted weekends, eight days and thirty days. I was in training. At one point, a group of potential directors from all over the land—priests and sisters mostly—came for an intense month-long experience in understanding the role of a Spiritual Director.. We became a close-knit group as we learned and allowed ourselves to be taught. I continued to do Life in the Spirit Seminars while being a part of this chosen group.

I met a sister from another St. Joseph Community. I was a sister of St. Joseph of Carondelet, founded in 1650 in Le Puy, France. As sisters came to America and landed in various states, they assumed the name of that region or state. Carondelet was the first to come and land in Carondelet, Missouri. Sisters went forth from there. She was a Sister of St. Joseph from Salina, Kansas. We were the same age and hit it off from the get-go. When the group participated in a retreat before the teaching began, I would find where she was sitting for a meal and sit next to her or vice versa. Sister Catherine and I became friends through the silence. Once we could talk, we already knew one another.

We were taught by some of the best theologians from Gonzaga University. We were like sponges, absorbing everything we could. At one point, we were given special assignments to accomplish. I was told that I was to give the homily at Mass the next day. That was my expertise. I was good at formulating my thoughts and speaking with a calm voice. One day wasn't very much time to prepare. I was a believer that after ten minutes, people stopped listening, so I told myself: *say what you want to say in that time and make it relevant.* I received many compliments, and my preaching/speaking career was launched.

We all received Spiritual Direction Certification by following the Spiritual Exercises of St. Ignatius, with certification awarded by Gonzaga University and Immaculate Heart Retreat Center. With this, we became certified spiritual directors. After that, I went through further training from my community and directed many of my sisters in a retreat setting.

At Catherine's invitation, I flew to Colorado and Kansas to give talks on the Gifts of the Spirit. I definitely knew this was my calling.

Chapter Eleven

We were a team that could not be split up!

My experiences were mounting. I was learning and growing daily, spiritually and professionally. I was happy. Except I felt that my relationship with Monsignor and Father Beno was getting uncomfortable. I did not "belong" to them. It was hard for them to treat me as an adult member of the staff. To them, I was the young sister who played the guitar. Their behavior became inappropriate. I shared my discomfort with Father Nigro, whom I trusted without question. He told me to consider leaving the Retreat House "while you can still pray."

Father George, the Pastor of St. Peter's parish, would come with Sister Lynda monthly for a day of prayer and discernment. I would watch them interact as a team. They had great respect for one another and worked well together for the good of the parish. I had shared with Lynda my confusion and discomfort with my relationship with the priests I worked with. There was, however, Father Ted, who came to the Retreat House at the same time I did.

He was a total gentleman and was fun to be around.

Father George offered me a position as the Parish Adult Education Coordinator if I decided to leave the Retreat House. I spoke with my superior and explained the situation, and she encouraged me to accept the offer.

Earlier in my stay at the Retreat House, my cousin Cheech bought me a car so I would have some independence. A brand-new VW Rabbit pulled up one day, and I was given the keys. It was a cream color with a bright orange stripe that ran along the sides. I had to ask permission from the community to use it. He registered it in the name of the Sisters of St. Joseph. My vow of poverty prevented me from owning it outright.

I was in heaven. My Rabbit and I took off every week on my day off. This did not set well with Monsignor, as I didn't have to ask permission to use the Retreat House car. I was free! I said goodbye to the staff and the sisters in the kitchen. Monsignor was out of town, and at five in the morning, in the pouring rain, I drove out, never to return.

I lived with Lynda's community at St. Anne's Infant Home. We had two rooms in the basement. Fanny was the lady who did the laundry for the home. She was a wonderful woman with a great sense of humor. I would often stop to chat with her on my way to my room.

One day, I said to her, "Fanny, who are 'they?'" People talk about "they."

She said in her wisdom, "Well, Sister, you say something important someday, and you can be 'they,' too."

I punched her playfully on the arm, and we both cracked up!

I lived with Lynda's Franciscan Sisters for a few years, until Evelyn, an elderly woman in the parish who worked closely with Lynda, decided to marry her first love, Ivan, who was a farmer in Montana. She asked Lynda and me if we would take her house and live in it rent-free. Wow, our very own home. We could decorate it and cook our own meals and come home to our own comfort, just the two of us. We jumped at the chance. We planted a garden out in the backyard. Being born and raised in Los Angeles, I did not know how things were grown. We each took a section of the garden and planted what we wanted. I was taken with the simplicity of how the little seeds turned into vegetables.

One day, I was out surveying my crops when I called Lynda and asked her to look at my radishes. She pulled one out, wiped it off, and took a bite. She said it was delicious. I looked perplexed because they were coming up one at a time. Lynda had been raised in Baker, Oregon, so she already knew how things grew.

She looked at me and began to laugh, "You thought they grew in a bunch?"

I said, "Yes, that's how they looked when we bought them at the store."

"With a twisty around them?" she said.

I realized, then, that I had a lot to learn about the food I ate and took for granted. This city girl was being educated in more ways than one.

I relished my time at St. Peter's. Father George was easy to work with. He was an exuberant preacher. He would walk around the altar and down the steps into the crowd and really bellow it out. He was not a tall man, but he was mighty.

Lynda had a beautiful voice. She was a Mezzo Soprano. So, she would sing various hymns at Christmas and Easter. This one time, she was to sing the "Exsultet," an Easter Vigil Proclamation at Holy Saturday services. That day, our electricity went out, and we had to fire up the lights before the evening service. She asked me to press a certain key on the organ, to give her the right note to begin singing. She glanced at me as the signal to press the note. I pressed, but no sound came out. She nodded again. I pressed, and nothing. Three times . . . nothing! Finally, in desperation, I hummed out a note. She was startled as I mimed:

"It's not working!"

She took it from there and sang a magnificent piece. I sat down in a heated sweat. The organ never recovered from the power outage.

We had many fun experiences during our time at St. Peter's. We made friends with families and would babysit for the Dauers when they needed a getaway. Three girls and a young boy. It was a weekend of firsts. I was glad that marriage was not in my future. Handling four kids was a test. Then Michael, the fifth one, came along!

Father George was transferred to a neighboring parish. As often happens, a new priest comes in and has his own way of doing things. Eventually, our positions were terminated and consolidated into one. One of us had to go. But we were a team that could not be split up, so we both left together.

We heard of a position in the Seattle Archdiocese west of the mountains. Two sisters were needed to work in twelve rural parishes. A team of two was moving down to the southern part of the state, and we were to take their place in the north. We were interviewed and got the position. Again, one door closed and another opened. The Holy Spirit at work.

Defiant Rosie

*Dad, Mom, Lou, me, and Cheech.
We were always together.*

Just the four of us! Early on!

Mom and Dad's engagement picture.

The Marin kids with Aunt Elsa. We grew up as one family.

Antonia and me as Postulants, 1963.

First home visit after taking first vows. I received the crucifix.

Brides of Christ, ready to receive the Holy Habit and a new name.

63

My guitar was a big part of my ministry.

First and fourth grade with the same class (above).
Up With People program (below).

Sister Carol and me. She has been my mentor since high school.

Rural Ministry North: Lynda and Rosie.
Rural Ministry South Virginia: Elizabeth and Lynda, too.

My graduation photo

My football book for women.

In my presider robe, ready for a wedding.

I am a portrait artist. My nephew Doug during three stages of his youth.

Our online profile pictures. The pictures that first attracted us to one another.

Mom and Dad blessing me before my wedding.

Our engagement picture. It was a part of our announcement.

My brother Lou.
Miss him every day.

Gary and Katie both played a special part in our wedding.

The three sisters. Hermanitas forever!

The Casa Woody Four: Aunt Elsa, Mom, Dad, and Aunt Grace. They lived together for more than 30 years.

My immediate family. So much love there!

Cheech, me, and Ron.

The McBride family.

Loving Midori. Rest in peace.

Ron's son Jimmy and family.

Collage: John (my lawyer),
Suzanne,
Mary Margaret, and Tina.

2nd collage
Renee (left); Michael
(upper right); and Annette
with her husband Jan.

A few of my Intercessory Prayer Group ladies.

Mom and Dad on their daily walk, hand in hand.

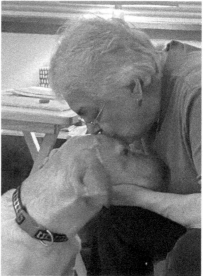

Blessing Jake, my special boy!

The Three Musketeers: Amy, me, and Katie.

From left: Jace, Oz, and Kailynn. They took exceptional care of my parents' personal needs during their final months.

After Mom's home memorial

Mom and Dad. Their love is now enduring into eternity.

Chapter Twelve

Our schedule was insane.

I remember thinking, *twelve parishes?* Working in one was challenging enough!

We were called Rural Ministry North and Rural Ministry South. It wasn't long until the four of us became lifelong friends. Sisters Virginia and Elizabeth, Sisters of Providence, became our mentors and guides as we tried to navigate the very complicated and demanding life of this new ministry. We traveled with them to a number of states to attend conferences that would be important to our ministry. They always came up with new adventures that would bring us together. Washington shores, St. Louise, New Orleans, Las Vegas, Yellowstone! They often instigated the adventures, and Lynda and I were more than happy to go along!

Sister Elizabeth passed several years ago. She and Virginia had ministered together for decades, and her loss was immense both to her and to us. She was a special part of our lives. We were Rural Ministry, and together, we made a difference!

As a team, we were responsible for training volunteers in several areas of parish life. We trained the Religious Education Coordinator, helped teachers with lesson plans for RE classes, and trained Parish Counsels, Liturgy Committees, Lectors, and Eucharistic Ministers. We were available for spiritual direction. We gave retreats and evenings of reflection. We worked closely with the priest in whatever areas he needed.

We spent a week in each county. In each county, there were as many as five parishes. We had to divide our time among them for the week: Skagit, Whatcom, and San Juan counties. When there was a fourth week in the month, it was spent in preparation for hitting the road the next month. We traveled down to the chancery office in Seattle once a month for meetings with our direct supervisor, as we were a part of the services provided by the Archdiocese.

The first year, we lived in a twenty-three-foot Prowler Trailer. We parked it in a parishioner's field in Whatcom County, so we could retire for some solitude and dinner before our evening sessions. Twenty-three feet may seem big, but for two of us to eat, sleep, shower, and be ready for our 8 AM appointment, it was not easy.

One night, after we finally managed to get our beds made up, we fell asleep only to be awakened by a loud noise. We jumped up and ran outside, not knowing if the whole trailer was about to explode. We found nothing, but we learned the next morning that a major pump had given out. We did not sleep well that night and were pretty ragged the next day. No breakfast or shower. Luckily, the man of the house was able to take care of the problem while we were at work. We laughed later, but not then!

We had our home in Skagit County and lived with families on the San Juan Islands. It was an exhausting ministry. We were glad for a fourth week. We could sleep in and take it slow for seven days, even while preparing for a new month. There was a contact person in each of the twelve parishes who was responsible for filling our time slots. We would meet with them to plan the following month's agenda. Sound overwhelming? It was!

Eventually, we sold the trailer and the Suburban that pulled it. We each had a small, economical car with a CB radio so we could communicate with each other, since we were rarely in the same place at the same time. This was before everyone had their own personal cell phone.

Meanwhile, I drove my VW Rabbit into the ground. I loved that car. It fit me perfectly! It died in Las Vegas while I was giving a training session for a parish. At one point, I was jumping the car, using a paperclip to spark the ignition. That was the clue that it was time to lay her to rest. I drove away in a new slate-gray Rabbit. Then I transferred my CB to the new car, and I was good to go. But I felt disloyal to my first car. She was a gift and an old friend.

Once we sold the trailer and car, we lost our solitude, because we then lived in parishioners' homes while ministering in their parish. We wouldn't get home until close to 11 PM sometimes, and they would be waiting up with hot chocolate, cookies, and a desire to chat. They were very kind and hospitable, but believe me, we just wanted to crawl in bed. Homemade breakfast was a treat, and we started our day with meetings by 8 AM.

On the San Juan Island, we would take the Red Eye ferry at 6 AM. I would go to Friday Harbor, the largest parish on San Juan Island, and Lynda would take Orcas and Lopez Islands, which meant that we would be in different lines at the ferry landing.

We had our CB antenna fixed to the top of our cars via a strong magnet. I was usually in the body of the ferry, as my island was the last to disembark. Lynda had to drive up the side ramp of the ferry that barely cleared the top of cars. I would always remind her to remove the antenna from her car, as it was too high. I would watch her climb the ramp, and sure enough, her antenna would snap off and hang lifeless on the side of her car. It never failed. She hadn't forgotten intentionally. She was always planning a retreat theme or some event that we were involved in. The antenna was the last thing on her mind!

We did this for eight years. Then our archbishop, Raymond Hunthausen, asked the four of us Rural Ministry sisters if we would consider taking on responsibility for several of the parishes we were already working in.

We asked, "What kind of responsibility, exactly?"

There was no priest available to pastor some parishes, and since we already had the respect of two of the parishes we work in, the archbishop said that he wanted to appoint us as Parochial Ministers, which are non-ordained Pastors. Lynda and I said we didn't think so. He asked again and then a third time. Finally, we couldn't keep denying his request. They were dissolving Rural Ministry, so we would be perfect for this new concept. The archbishop had faith in the four of us. My faith was not as strong as his.

Chapter Thirteen

A Miracle? You tell me!

Cannon Law—the principles and guidelines that govern the Church—says that parishes must be led by an ordained priest. We did not have enough priests to pastor our rural parishes. So, the archbishop had to make some decisions and become creative in providing competent leadership to parishes.

The team concept was created. An ordained priest would oversee all parishes and ensure that the sacraments were available. Our team consisted of two priests, a deacon, Lynda, and me. On Sundays and Saturdays, we would rotate ministers, so that a Mass was said at each church for at least one of the weekend Masses. If the parish only had one Mass, then alternately, I would conduct a Communion Service. Laypeople were trained to give out Communion on weekdays if no priests were available, but on a weekend, it was different.

I was responsible for doing the schedule that would tell each of the team members where they would go on

Saturday and Sunday. It was a puzzle, because for some weekends, a team member might be on vacation or otherwise not be around. Then what? I didn't dare have a Communion Service two weekends in a row in a given parish. It was a juggling act. It was hard having Lynda and me responsible for two parishes together. After one year, Lynda returned to Spokane to re-create her spirit. I continued on without her for the remainder of our commitment. I missed her. We had been a team for fifteen years.

I presided at a Communion Service every weekend at one of the five parishes in our valley. Sometimes, more than one. I would preach as many as five times on a given weekend. If Father was at my parish, I would be officiating a Communion Service at another parish. These services had all the components of the Mass, except the consecration. Only Father could do that. A priest would consecrate enough hosts (small round wafers) for me to use at my services. I would offer a prayer of Thanksgiving and Praise in place of the consecration and then distribute Communion or sit while two Eucharistic Ministers gave out Communion.

One Sunday during the summer, as I was presiding at a service at a neighboring church, we ran out of hosts for Communion. Father had forgotten to consecrate enough for my service. I went to get the hosts, and when I looked inside the ceramic container, I saw only three hosts and some small pieces. The church was full, as there were people visiting.

The visitors were already surprised to see me on the altar. And now, there was not enough for everyone to receive Communion.

I told the Eucharistic Ministers of my dilemma. "I told the congregation that this is where I feel my inadequacy," I said. "In the back room, the sacristy, there was a plastic bag full of hosts that are unconsecrated. But I can't do it. So now you will have to go without because Father forgot."

I instructed the Eucharistic Ministers to break the hosts into tiny pieces and see how far it would go. I sat while the music played, and people approached for Communion. My eyes were closed as I prayed that there would be another miracle of the loaves. Finally, everyone who approached received a tiny piece, and there were a few pieces left over.

I shared with the congregation what had just happened, and the church erupted in applause! A miracle? You tell me! I was hugged and thanked and told that I was doing a great service to the parish, and they didn't understand why I just couldn't go back there and get the hosts. It didn't matter that I wasn't a priest. What mattered was their right to receive the Eucharist. Another teachable moment. The Holy Spirit at work again!

Deacon George Peterson would also preside at Communion Services. However, he was able to officiate at weddings and baptisms, and we both could preside at funeral vigils and graveside services. He was my go-to guy when I needed help validating a marriage (that is, marrying a couple in the church after their annulment was complete). I was a trained advocate for annulments. He trusted me to have the appropriate paperwork completed, and we would do it together.

Being an ordained deacon, he had a wife and a family. He embodied kindness and understanding. He has since passed, and my world is without his love and compassion.

I'm not going to lie. Not everyone was happy with my appointment and some made it obvious. I would have people say things like, "Don't take this personally, Sister, but we wish you weren't here." People would walk out as soon as they realized it was a Communion Service and not a Mass. On the rare occasion that I was at one of my parishes with a priest, I would preach. Some would get up and go to the back of the church so they wouldn't have to listen to me. Yet, if I wasn't there, the doors would be closed. I was keeping the parish going. It was very stressful, and some who loved me when I worked as a rural ministry sister turned on me when I became their parochial minister. Some felt punished because they didn't get a priest, when in reality I was the one being punished. I was just sure I would fly into heaven, having made up for my sins here on earth.

I completely felt my limitations when it came to the sacraments. I couldn't offer Mass. I couldn't hear confessions (though I heard many). I couldn't baptize or anoint the sick. Only an ordained priest could do that, and we didn't have one in our parish. Yet, I was responsible for the spiritual growth of the parish. I received nasty letters and phone messages. Granted, only a small percentage made their anger known, but it was enough and it was constant.

In a male-dominated Church, it is difficult for a woman to carve her place without conflict or resentment. But I tried. And in the process, I met with some opposition. I did everything I could to fulfill those duties. I was better than no one at all . . . but not as good as a priest. Very frustrating years for me. Despite the obstacles, I learned a lot and believed that God was indeed calling me to something greater than myself. Besides, strumming my guitar on a street corner was always an option!

There were very few women doing what I was doing in my Church at the time. We were being interviewed by people who were writing their thesis, as well as newspaper articles, about the concept of women in this ministry. But no one truly understood the pain that struck me inwardly, day after day, while trying to fulfill my role as the Spiritual Head of two parishes. This was history in the making! I was either going to succeed or end up like Joan of Arc, tied to a tree after passing out the matches!

One day, a journalist called and asked if she could follow me around for a weekend and see firsthand what I did. I thought, *why not? Finally, someone who can give an accurate account of this new concept.*

She came on Saturday in time for the 5 PM service. It was a Communion Service, and I was presiding. *Perfect,* I thought*, she can see how sacred the ritual is and how prayerful it remains in the absence of a priest.* I felt hopeful that she would write about this in a way that would give credibility to my ministry as a woman.

I changed into my white robe, which was fashioned just for a woman. On my left shoulder hung a banner. I had many different colors that corresponded to the seasons of the liturgical year. Two women made me beautiful banners as the robe came with only a red, white, and blue banner. The ones made for me were exquisite in their embroidered detail and elegant fabrics.

I was chastised by a parishioner for trying to act and dress like a priest. And yet, what I wore, no priest would be caught dead in!

I processed in, as usual, to music and song. I did the opening prayers just as in a Mass. I preached and offered a prayer of Thanksgiving and Praise, standing to the side of the altar, not behind. And when it came time for Communion, I went to the Tabernacle and got the glass container with the consecrated hosts. A trained Eucharistic Minister, along with myself, gave out Communion while the choir sang. The service ended with the usual, "Go in peace to love and serve the Lord," and I processed out.

We had a dinner in the hall, served by our Knights of Columbus men in the parish, which was perfect because the reporter could then circulate and interview parishioners and get their feelings about this new form of ministry. I was aware that she would no doubt pick up some negativity from those who did not like it, but I had no control over that.

When she left that evening, she said she would not come back for the Sunday service. She had enough information already. She promised to send me her article before it went to press. She wrote for syndicated newspapers, so her article would go nationwide. Even better, as it was important for people to understand what the Church was having to do to provide quality service in the absence of a priest. I slept well that night with a heavy sigh of relief.

We were heading into the Easter Triduum Holy Thursday, Good Friday, and Holy Saturday, all leading up to Easter Sunday. Lots of rituals to prepare for and a different homily for each day. On Holy Saturday, I received a call from the chancery office of the archbishop in Seattle. One of the priests had seen the morning paper featuring the article about me and my ministry. The reporter had promised that I could read it before it went to press, but she never sent it to me.

The entire article was false. She said that I had elevated the host and the wine like Father does at Mass. She had sat right in front and saw that there was no wine and that the hosts were already consecrated. This priest asked me what in the world was I doing. I tried to explain. He said he would not give the paper to the archbishop or remove that section. That article went all over the United States, and I got hate mail from coast to coast.

I tracked down the author and found her in New York at her parents' home. She did not try to explain herself; all she said was that she wrote what she saw. I was angry, but worse, I felt betrayed. She could have made a big difference had she been honest. Again, my hands were tied, and I had no recourse to defend myself. I had no control over where the article landed. I knew then that I was not the one to blaze this trail. Miraculously, it died down with minimal damage, except for the ones who were threatening to lynch me if they ever met me. By that time, I would have gladly supplied the rope!

When approached by my archbishop to consider this position, I knew there was a reason why we said no three times. Something deep inside of me had a feeling that this would not end well.

One day, while I was counseling a parishioner, I started to feel sick. I told him I needed to bring our time to an end and maybe we could talk again another day. I went home and took a shower, thinking it would make me feel better. It didn't. I called my doctor and told her my symptoms. She told me to come in now. She took an EKG and sent me to the emergency room, as I was having a heart attack. After several days in the ICU, one of the priests came in and gave me the anointing of the sick. I remember thinking, *I am not going to die for this.* Though, I felt like this was it!

My community advised me to take three months off to recuperate and rest. The stress of trying to please everyone had gotten the best of me. I rested, prayed, and got help from both a counselor and my spiritual director. I discerned that I would not renew my contract for another term. I would ask my community for a sabbatical year. I needed to figure things out. Usually, a sabbatical is time for a person to travel or perhaps continue toward a degree, or to otherwise retool in some way. I wanted to do nothing. I was exhausted from years of trying to be good enough for the people in my care. To some, I never was!

Mercifully, that heart attack offered me the perfect opportunity to stop, slow down, and take inventory. Otherwise, I likely would have just pressed on until the outcome had been much worse.

Chapter Fourteen

Deacon George, are you free Friday evening?

I completed my term and told the people at Mass one Sunday. Father Paul was there because he knew I was going to make an announcement. After Mass, when announcements were usually made, I stood up at the podium and told them I was not going to seek a second term. I had just returned from my sick leave, and so they knew I was in a fragile state.

I was surprised at the reaction. After Mass, as we were greeting people while they left through the doors of the church, I was stopped and told by many that they were sorry to see me go. They said I was one of the best pastors they had ever had. They found my homilies informative, with practical suggestions for living a good life. I got hugged and told I would be missed! Huh? Where were they when I was being told that I wasn't really wanted there? Most were content and didn't know what I was experiencing on a daily basis.

As astounding as it was to hear this, I felt vindicated in a way. My time was not wasted. I did make a difference in their lives, at least for most of them. My second parish was a little different. Most were sad to see me go, but many who had had a more difficult time with my ministry were glad.

Since I also offered Communion Services and preached in three other parishes, I had to share my decision with them as well. The other parishes had always shown compassion and acceptance of me. I wasn't their parochial minister. They had a priest or a deacon, and that was more acceptable. I received the same response from the other parishes. They were sorry to see me go. They enjoyed my Communion Services and my preaching. I felt loved and humbled.

I still had a few months before I was scheduled to leave. Ironically, my Communion Services were well attended, and almost no one walked out. I prepared my homilies like always. I made sure that my message was pertinent to the scripture readings of the day and that there was something they could relate to and carry with them throughout the week. I would spend hours in preparation.

Since I was one of two advocates trained in the annulment process, I tried to complete as many as possible before I left. Annulments are truly misunderstood. When a couple marries in the Church, they still need to get a civil license, so that the marriage is recorded in the state. They present the license to the priest to sign, and then they fill out the appropriate paperwork, so the Church can witness that the marriage is valid as a sacrament. This involves two different processes: one civil and the other a sacrament.

When a couple divorces, they go through a process to

dissolve the civil marriage. That does not negate the validity of any children born during the marriage. The annulment process is to dissolve the sacramental marriage. Again, that doesn't negate the validity of the children born during the marriage. The confusion is that people think an annulment says the marriage never happened. Instead, it acknowledges that it took place as a sacrament within the Church, but now that sacrament is dissolved.

At one point, I had forty-two annulments going on at once. There are at least six kinds of annulments. Some are issued within weeks, and others may take years, as they are more involved.

I had a couple come to me at their wit's end. For years, they had been trying to get an annulment and have their marriage blessed by the Church. It's called a con-validation—valid civilly and sacramentally.

They came to me seeking help. They had recently moved from another state. They got no help from their former pastor; he may have been too busy, as starting the process demands a lot of hands-on hours with the couple. There is some spiritual healing that may be needed, so the advocate (me) may need to spend some time in counseling to help resolve past hurts. This couple came to see me. I listened to their frustration and felt sorry for the lack of compassion shown to them over the years.

I finally asked two questions: Was their former spouse still living? They both responded, "No." Did they have proof of their deaths, an obituary, or a letter from family? They said they could come up with something and bring it in.

I excused myself and went out to make a phone call to Deacon George. He knew when he heard from me during working hours that something was up! As a deacon, he was ordained and could witness marriages.

"Are you free this Friday evening to witness a marriage?" I asked, explaining the situation, saying that I would provide the necessary paperwork and have it ready for his signature.

He trusted that I knew what I was doing. He was free that evening.

I returned to the couple and said, "Since your former spouses are deceased, there is no need for a formal annulment. This is very simple and can be resolved in a few days."

They were speechless. No priest had ever asked them if their former spouses were living. I went through extensive training with the Archdiocese to know enough to ask those questions.

"If you're free this Friday evening, Deacon George will con-validate (bless) their marriage," I told the couple. "Then you'll be free to receive the sacraments in the Church."

They both sat there and cried. Then they brought me the necessary papers, and I filled out what was needed from the church. They notified their children, and we had a simple yet meaningful celebration. George was a compassionate man of God. He came to my rescue many times. I miss him in my world.

I was given a wonderful, heartfelt goodbye celebration in the parish hall. It was packed with people from other parishes. I received gifts and cards and a whole lot of hugs.

There were tears and laughter shared, and I left at the end of the year. I truly wished only blessings upon the people who were in my care. They were caught between something new and something old and familiar. I knew that there was a lot of healing that would need to take place in the coming year.

Chapter Fifteen

I was glad for the year to sort things out!

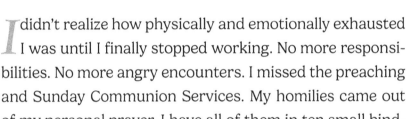

I didn't realize how physically and emotionally exhausted I was until I finally stopped working. No more responsibilities. No more angry encounters. I missed the preaching and Sunday Communion Services. My homilies came out of my personal prayer. I have all of them in ten small binders. They are like a diary of my thoughts and prayers, and I look through them every now and then.

I slept a lot the first few days. I had many friends who checked on me periodically, but for the most part, I just kept to myself. I did see a counselor and reconnected with my spiritual director. I regrouped my thoughts and started to heal. I had a lot of time to reflect and remember. Memories would flood my waking moments, and my anger would flood me again. A big parish meeting was called and open to whoever wanted to attend. They pretty much raked me over the coals because I was going to have a child baptized whose parents weren't married. Did I realize what a scandal that would be? Suppose a person leaned over to the person next to them and told them the parents weren't married.

I tried to defend my reasoning. First, the scandal would be that the person felt the need to gossip and share information they had no business sharing. Second, Cannon Law says that all the parents have to do is ask for that sacrament on behalf of their child, and then the priest was obligated to baptize the child. Turning them away would have been the greater sin, in my opinion. The priest present sat there in silence. I was facing mean-spirited people looking to trip me up and get me removed. I volleyed back to them their insults and held my ground. I was being arraigned and sentenced all at once.

Memories like these flooded my waking hours. I knew I didn't deserve that treatment, and I shared as much with my counselor. She agreed and cautioned me to try and let go of my anger, as it would only serve to hurt me, not them. I was glad for the year to sort things out. I didn't have to deal with negativity anymore. I read the cards I had received at my going away party. They were like balm to my soul.

I was attempting to clarify things for myself. A big question arose. Did I want to continue to fight the established Church? Women were always going to be second best to the priest. I knew God was calling me to do more than clean the church after a wedding while Father took pictures with the bride and groom. He got the stipend handed to him in thanksgiving for "marrying them." I did all the prep work, and he signed the papers. I told myself,

"Let it go, Rosie, don't make yourself sick."

It was months before I felt like I could start over in some viable way. My provincial superior came to visit and see how I was doing. I loved Joyce. I had directed her during her eight-day retreat one summer. I knew her soul. She was kind and compassionate, traits I looked for in a person. I shared that I was struggling with my future. I had been in the community for more than thirty years at that time. The best parts of my youth and early adult life were behind me. I was tired and afraid of what was in front of me.

She listened without interruption. I think she knew where I was going with all this. She stayed with me for several days. We went to dinner and watched some TV. I had a little fourteen-inch black and white that I hardly ever watched. We talked a lot. Finally, I had a moment of peace come over me. I know enough about discernment to seek your peace level when trying to come to a decision. Peace is where God meets you. Being able to talk things out is helpful. Once you hear yourself, then you can look at what you are saying and come to conclusions. Another person's view is crucial.

Finally, before she left, we had a moment of prayer together. She wanted me to be healed from the hurts of my former ministries. She wanted God to open doors for me that would allow my gifts in ministry to be appreciated. As she spoke, I knew what my next steps should be.

I said through tears, "I think I am being called to leave the community and find a way to minister without constraints."

She wasn't shocked, as our conversation had been approaching that decision, and she knew it.

"I understand how you came to that decision and I'll support you in it," she said, "but I'm terribly sad to lose someone like you who is trying to foster women in the Church ministry."

"The Church is not ready for someone like me," I said, "and I can't wait around for them to recognize our importance."

My provincial superior suggested that I begin a three-year period of what is called "Exclaustration." This is a church term, meaning a sort of leave of absence. In that three-year period, my goal was to see if I was able to live as a laywoman in the world. I had left home at seventeen and was now approaching my fifties. I had no job. No bank account. No credit. What a leap of faith this was going to be.

I was scared, but my peace level told me this was right. The community would continue to keep my health insurance active. I could use the car as before. These years were only a test. I could return to the community at the end or seek a final dispensation from my vows through Rome.

We hugged. She blessed me and off she went.

Chapter Sixteen

For the first time, I questioned God's benevolence.

What have I done?
I felt alone with no direction, except I knew that God was calling me to something new. I had to figure out how I was going to live. I had been renting this great home for the past fifteen years. Lynda and I had lived there and created many memories. She was gone now, and I was on my own.

I couldn't use the title "Sister" anymore. *So, how will "Rosie" manage?* When Lynda and I were together, we had to pro-rate our budget and give our communities an idea of how much money we would need to live on that year. They would put a monthly amount in a joint checking account, and we would try to live within those means. Each community paid into the account.

We found furniture from an abandoned convent in the area. We got twin beds and a sofa, as well as a table and chairs. We kept an eye out for other things like dressers, end tables for our bedrooms, and a coffee table for the front room. We found plates and pans, and somehow we were able to get the rest of what we needed. Friends also gave us things they thought we could use.

Our little house was eclectic. Nothing matched. Therefore, everything matched. Our landlords lived next door, so they were helpful when things broke or when grass needed mowing. We were an enigma to them. They took great pride in caring for us. A little too much sometimes.

When Lynda left my community, I bought out her portion. The contents of the house became mine. I still had to pay the rent. Friends would, without me asking, send me money. I was able to live from their goodness while looking for a job. My method was to approach the various parishes and say that I would work on their many annulments if I could be hired on an hourly basis. It was a hard sell, but eventually, when they realized how many annulments I had going throughout the valley, they had to say yes or do them themselves. This was a step toward personal independence. It wasn't much, but by then I was used to living on a shoestring.

My job description grew as parish needs became apparent. I was a spiritual director and managed to pick up individuals that the priest didn't have time for. Things were working out well, and I was able to open a bank account in my name and even get a personal credit card. I had to prove that I could do this.

In a way, this newfound freedom was exhilarating. For the first time in my life, I was on my own. I could do what I wanted and go where I wanted without getting permission.

At the end of the three years, I petitioned Rome to be dispensed from my vows. I signed the appropriate papers, and I was totally on my own.

The community let me keep the car I was driving and gave me a loan. The car died shortly after, and that loan had to go toward a used car. I knew many people by that time and approached Jack Gubrud, who owned a car dealership, for help. He found just the one for me within my price range. He and his wife Claudette were my guardian angels. When I could finally afford to buy the house I was renting, they co-signed for me. This was the Holy Spirit's intervention once again.

I had befriended Tina, a single mom who had two small boys. She worked with our parish youth. It was easy to just be myself with her. I had my personal space, but she became a friend to do things with. Her boys, Justin and Jordan, were five and three years old when I first met her, and they had found a place in my heart. They call me Auntie Rosie to this day. She remarried and had two more children, Jayson and Anna. Sadly, she lost her life in a tragic accident. At the time, her youngest were five and three.

I had never known such pain, and for the first time, I questioned God's benevolence. *How could this happen?* I flew to Arizona and officiated her service and eulogized her at the Mass here in the valley. The pain in her young children's eyes was sometimes too much for me. I took them into my home as often as I could. We would talk about their mom and pray together. They needed to say what their little hearts were feeling. My home and my love gave them the space to do that. They are grown now, but her loss still sits in my heart.

I was getting along well and was able to pay my rent when, as often happens, a new priest was assigned to the parish I was working in. He was young and was assigned as Parish Administrator, not Pastor, as it was his first assignment. He was transitioning from an order priest (a Benedictine) to a diocesan priest, and he had to wait for the proper time to pass before he could assume the position of Pastor.

He was having a hard time adjusting and found me a threat to his position. I was well-known and established, and he was new and trying to find his way. Supposedly, I was in his way. It didn't work out, and eventually I left. *Now what?* Well, for one thing, all the annulments were now on his desk.

While in my parochial minister role, I worked closely with the local funeral home. Lemley Chapel was the funeral home of choice for many of my parishioners. I conducted vigil services and graveside services. Anything that wasn't a Mass, I could do. Eventually, Lemley's began to call on me to do funerals for anyone who did not have a formal church to turn to. I became like one of the staff, and the funeral directors Rick and Chuck were like family.

I was also on call at other funeral homes in the valley. Kern's was a family-owned funeral home, and I became one of the regulars for them as well. The funeral directors— Connie and her son Jeremiah—treated me like I was one of the staff. In both places, I got along well with the other employers. I was glad for the experience, and the money helped, too.

Quite by accident, I happened to be reading a Catholic newspaper and saw a small ad that said, and I am paraphrasing now, "If you are wanting to be in ministry and are looking for a community to share it with, contact us—The Federation of Christian Ministries." I contacted them and became a member. I wanted a faith-filled group behind me as I ministered, much like my religious community was for me. I didn't want to be out there on my own. After a few months, I petitioned to become a certified member. With certification came the privilege of witnessing state-approved weddings. I could continue to do funerals as called upon, and I could even officiate Christian baptisms. I wrote a paper on how I saw myself in this new role and was accepted for certification.

I was truly in my element, doing what I felt called to do. The Church couldn't touch me, as I was not acting as a member of the Catholic Church, but as a chaplain. I had all the requirements. *Now, how to get myself out there for people to know what I can do.* The Spirit was leading me. I got a call from our local hospice asking if I would be interested in a chaplain position! One of the chaplains had attended a funeral I had done and recommended me to the director. I pulled together my resume and got letters of recommendation. I took a copy of my master's diploma, and off I went to the interview.

I was floating on air. I did well in the interview and was told that they would look no further and that I had the job!

A real position in a viable ministry. With benefits!

I was so elated to finally have a paying position. I knew that this was a door that opened because the Spirit had moved me in this new direction.

At the same time, to help supplement my income, I was in direct ministry with my lawyer, John. He was another person whom the Spirit had brought back into my life at precisely the right time for both of us. This happened after I was in an auto accident that totaled my car and messed up my knee. I was not at fault, but it was part of a chain reaction.

I turned to John for legal help. I had to get a new used car. Since I now had a paying position, I had insurance and was able to put a down payment on an SUV. I wanted a lot more car around me this time, to surround and protect me. John went to bat for me with an under-insured motorist claim. The person who had hit me had to pay. We went to mediation.

"Don't say a word," he told me. "I'll do all the talking with the mediator."

I sat in stone silence while his lawyer skills went to work. We walked out of the deliberations with enough for me to pay off my car and put money in an annuity. He was smart, gentle, and very knowledgeable.

On the way home, he asked me if I would do him a favor.

"Of course!" I said. "You just saved my future!"

He shared that he had been working with victims of priest abuse. Specifically, a priest who had ministered in our valley several years ago. The women were distraught, and he wondered if I would meet with them in a spiritual direction capacity. Maybe informally over lunch. I agreed and met with the women individually after he introduced us.

I heard their stories and was saddened, both for them and for the Church I had given my life to. John and I would meet often to collaborate and stay on course. Since I had firsthand knowledge of where to find things at the chancery level (the archdiocese offices), I was able to tell him who to contact for the information he might need. We worked together to help these ladies. I had once been treated inappropriately by two priests and could understand their hurt and confusion. This gave me a huge advantage in helping them to heal.

When John and I would meet, I could tell that this was taking a toll on him. He was Catholic and working with the legal team from the church, trying to advocate for the women in his care. However, going up against the Catholic Church was a David and Goliath scenario. I was there to support him as well as the women he was representing. I watched this faith-filled man navigate through the bureaucracy of the Church. Helpless to change things, but knowing he was a man of integrity who allowed the Spirit to guide him, I watched him work late hours to find the right means of financial support for the victims.

Eventually, his health told him enough was enough. He needed to retire and turn the rest over to God. His body finally gave in, and my friend and confidant passed away at a too-young age. I visited him a few days before he died. He was in a care facility. I sat by his bed and talked to him, even though he was unresponsive. He needed to know what a wonderful man he was, and how he had helped hundreds, if not thousands, of people in his life. I reminded him that God was waiting to embrace him and thank him for being such a good and faithful servant. I blessed him one last time.

It was my privilege to officiate his funeral service. The service was attended by so many friends in the community. I can hardly believe he's gone. My heart misses him every day. He was sent to be a special part of my life. To teach me tolerance and how to live a life of integrity. Rest peacefully now, my friend, until we meet again.

Chapter Seventeen

Life events directly impact our sense of God.

Hospice was a totally new experience. I mean, I understood the concept: terminal illness, six months or less to live. I realized this was sacred ground, and I was going to be moved and changed in ways I never knew.

I worked with some amazing people. Nurses, social workers, CNAs (certified nursing assistants), chaplains, and volunteers. I always said that you needed a "hospice heart" to do this work, or ministry, as I believed it to be. It took a special type of person to really be present for the terminally ill, and I was privileged to be among many of them. Many are my closest friends to this day. You can't be surrounded by death and dying all day and not be impacted by the reality of it.

During my second interview with Ashford Radio, I was asked to expand on the topic of my experience with hospice. Many of the things that happen to us over our lifetime, I believe, directly impact our sense of God. And I wanted to use my experience as a hospice chaplain to illustrate that concept.

Several years ago, I retired from hospice. During my thirteen years in that ministry, I had the privilege of accompanying men, women, and, sadly, sometimes young children during their final months of life. It is very humbling to be in this position. When you are faced with your impending death, for the most part, there is no more pretense. Life is what it is. Self-evaluation sets in for some. Depression for others. Everyone is trying to make sense of it all.

I have listened to some fascinating life reviews. People want to tell their stories, not just for my edification, but largely because telling them somehow validates all of their accomplishments. They hear themselves talk, and that gives me the opportunity to ask questions and affirm the good that I hear. Many searched my face as they spoke, looking for that affirmation.

Not all patients are able to articulate their feelings. Some are unresponsive and are just barely holding on to the last bit of life left in them. That is when I lean over them and speak gently into their ear and remind them:

"There is more to you than the worst thing you've ever done," I say. "God finds you where you are and loves you there."

Those who can talk and actually want a chaplain visit are eager to pour their hearts out.

Some speak with a tone of regret, wishing they had done things differently, wishing they had been kinder and more present to their children and spouse. Some have regrets for dreams unfulfilled. Many are angry because of the difficult and heart-wrenching events in their lives. Examples include the tragic loss of their spouse, or the death of a child years ago. Some remain angry at God for those events that drastically changed the course of their lives.

I have been confronted by some who asked me to try and talk them out of their anger, to prove to them that there is a God who cares. Some had allowed me into their lives just to level those confrontations at me and see me squirm. But my role as a chaplain was not to try to convert them or change their minds, to or plead God's case. As a chaplain, I enter into their lives right where they are, and I listen. I sometimes cry with them and feel their anger and pain, all the while I am praying inwardly that they will experience peace before they die, and that I will be given the proper words to help them achieve that.

There is an internal struggle that often takes place when dealing with end-of-life issues. Some of the people I ministered to as a chaplain had been estranged from their Church for whatever reason. It is not my position to try and make sense of their anger for them. I'm there just to be a spiritual presence in their lives at this point and perhaps to try to help them come to some kind of peaceful resolution, which may involve self-forgiveness or reconciliation with a person or event.

I remember a particular gentleman who allowed me into his home, more than anything just because he was curious. I arrived at his home at our agreed-upon time. He was terminally ill, but he was still able to interact well. He would be seated on his couch, waiting for my visit.

It became apparent early on in my time with him that he was enjoying asking me deep theological questions that were difficult to answer. For example:

"How can we be sure that there are three persons in one God?"

Or "Prove to me that Jesus was Divine as well as Human." *Are you kidding me?*

"How do you know that God even exists?"

Ha! What? I make it a personal point never to debate religion or politics! No one wins. You just get heated up trying to make your point, not really listening to the other's point of view. I don't mind discussing it, but I will not argue to prove a point.

He used to get frustrated with me because I would answer him with the simplest of reasoning:

"I don't know" or "it's a mystery to me too."

It was never good enough, by golly, as he would slam his fist down on the arm of the couch.

Throughout my hour-long visit, or sometimes two hours, I would be praying inwardly that God would touch him in some way. It became obvious to me that he was carrying around a lot of anger and, understandably, leveling it all on God through me.

Despite our conversation, we would end our time together with mutual respect and some laughter. His wife, who was a devout Christian, would be standing in the kitchen or by the hallway, clasping her hands and fidgeting in nervous concern for what he would say next that might offend me. I would glance at her periodically to assure her,

"I got this," even though I knew I clearly didn't! Eventually, my time would be up, and, mercifully, I could leave.

Once, early on in our visits, when I got up to leave, he said to me rather sarcastically, "Aren't you going to pray with me or give me a blessing or do something that chaplains are supposed to do?"

Now, this was coming from a man who said he was a confirmed agnostic, which is someone who is unsure whether God exists, refuses to declare belief in the existence or nonexistence of God, or is a skeptic who does not believe one way or the other (in contrast, an atheist is someone who does not believe in the existence of any deity whatsoever).

When I responded, I did not say anything like, "Ha, finally!" Instead, I placed my hands on his head and said, "I hope that you will come to a peaceful resolution in your heart on whether or not there is a God who loves you."

Then, without thinking, I traced a cross on his forehead and said, "God bless you." And I gently tapped him on his nose!

Oh, what have I done?

His wife winced!

I gulped.

He looked at me, disbelieving. "Did you just sock me in the nose?"

I did some fast talking!

This was my signature blessing that I had used since visiting my first patient. It was something I had learned as a child from my parents. They called this loving tap a "beep." They used to bless us when we went to bed, then even as adults when we visited and left, or before any special occasion. They would trace the cross on our foreheads and say, "God bless you." One day, my dad added another simple yet endearing touch by beeping us on the nose after the crossing.

"What was that for?" I had asked my dad.

"It locks it in!"

To this day, people say, "Rosie, please beep me!" They know it's part of a blessing.

Well, I was used to doing that with permission to other patients, and I had done it to my agnostic patient without thinking . . . beep and all! I immediately felt as if I had crossed a line that was not mine to cross. I started to apologize, and he grabbed my arm.

"No, don't," he said. "That was sweet."

I exhaled and left him at that point, praying in gratitude as I drove to my next appointment.

I remember asking God to work through me to touch him in whatever way would be most effective for him. One time, our visit had gone so long that I was running late into my next appointment. I left without giving him the "cross and beep," as we had come to call the blessing. When I arrived the next week, his wife met me at the door and told me that he was upset that whole day, because I had not blessed him before I left. He also let me know that it hadn't sat well with him, and he asked me not to leave without cross-and-beeping him again!

"I promise I won't," I said. "Please remind me each visit." Inwardly, I was smiling.

I continued to see him weekly for well over a year. He still had a terminal illness, and he never improved enough to become discharged from hospice care. Every week, as I drove to see him, I would pray, "Oh, Lord, I don't know what to expect today, just speak through me."

Over the months, he tried not to waver in his beliefs or non-beliefs, but I knew differently. Until one day, I got a call from his wife that he had taken a sharp decline during the night. It was not my scheduled time to see him, but I went immediately to his home. He was now in a hospital bed in the front room, sitting up on the edge of the bed with his oxygen on, gasping for air. I had noticed his recent decline and asked his hospice social worker to order the bed, to provide more comfort for him and ease for his wife.

However, I had not expected to see him in that state so quickly. I stood in front of him, putting my hands on his shoulders. He leaned his head against my heart and said through labored breathing:

"Rosie, there has got to be an easier way."

I tilted his head up to meet my eyes, took a chance, and said, "There is . . . how about we take your mustard seed faith and hook it on to mine and let me pull you over!"

He knew what I meant, as I had seen little bits of acceptance creep into our conversations over the last few months. I never commented on it and just let God work. After I made that suggestion of letting my faith pull him over, he looked at me and said, "Okay." It was a weak "okay," but an okay nonetheless.

I prayed a simple prayer for peace, acceptance, and forgiveness, gave him a final cross and beep, and gently laid him back in his bed.

I stayed with him, holding his hand until his breathing changed, and he appeared to be resting comfortably. I gave a hug and a blessing to his wife.

"Call me if he becomes agitated and wants me to be with him," I said.

There were tears in her eyes, and she thanked me for "pulling him over into the Lord's arms."

I left knowing that he was in God's care and that my work with him was done. My friend died later that evening. I had to let him go. I had grown to love him and respect his journey. It was not up to me to change his mind or convince him to believe the way I did. I had given that job back to God a long time ago.

I had merely been there as a presence in his life: To meet him precisely at that moment in time and to join him on his walk, to listen and encourage and show not in words so much, but by my behavior, that he was lovable and cherished and forgiven no matter what. I hope I was a blessing to him.

I think I was, but he was also a blessing to me as well. Because he was in my life, with all of his questions and challenges, I was forced to reevaluate, once again, my beliefs and allow God to move in me at the same time that I was ministering to him. I was once again faced with my doubts and personal questions about God's existence. His questions and life stories triggered memories of some of my own experiences. I had to practice active listening and not jump in to try and prove a point or make him "see the light" and take away his pain and confusion. I got a hefty dose of "tolerance" thrown at me, and I gently let the Holy Spirit work in me and through me.

Since then, there have literally been hundreds of meaningful encounters like that during my thirteen years with hospice. Each encounter is unique, but every person has deepened my concept of God and taught me more about living and dying than any book I could ever read. Everyone's journey is different, but all of us are impacted by significant events and people throughout our years. We can't help it. That's just life. Much of what we experience in life helps us live well. Other experiences tempt us to go against what we know to be right, and we live with the unsettled feelings that they leave us with. It sits in our hearts and subconsciousness, causes stress in later years, and comes to the forefront when we are faced with our final months, weeks, or days of life.

When all is said and done, the most important thing I have discovered is that a person wants to be reassured that their life has meaning, and that, in the end, it was all worth it. I remind them that God's love for us surpasses all understanding. That we don't have to be good to receive God's love. God's love makes us good. And then, I let them go, and God takes it from there. And I am changed in some way. My concept of God has either been tested, enriched, or both.

I have been taught by both the simplest of people and by those who have multiple degrees hanging on their walls. And in any given week, that last visit may have been repeated several times. Each person whose final months I have been privileged to be a part of touches me and changes me in some way.

Every book we read, movie we see, person we talk to, and disaster we watch on TV or newscast impacts us without us even knowing it. And if we are spiritual at all, we formulate an image of God that's somehow related to the event. There are some people who come into our lives who touch us at our very soul and move us to express love. We know that their very presence has made a difference in our lives, hopefully for good.

If we live to be a good old age and look over our life, we can see the peaks and valleys, both when God was tangible, or, in our mind, when He was missing in action. Listening to the stories of the dying brings that home very clearly. And I was the one who got to affirm their goodness and reassure them that all of those peaks and valleys were part of their particular journey to this point in time. As I remind them, I also remind myself of the same.

I have been living in the Skagit Valley in Western Washington since 1981, and the people know me and respect my ministry. I have been a part of the lives of the people here, from the birth of a child to the death of a loved one. And each event has had a tremendous effect on my life, and I have been changed because of them all.

Chapter Eighteen

What do you want me to do for you?

I remember, as a little girl growing up, my family would gather once a week at night to pray the Rosary. I had a child's understanding of that prayer, but I did not yet fully grasp why exactly we were offering the prayer for, say, a close friend, or for someone in the family who was ill. In school, we would pray for world peace or for a need that another student would bring to our attention. I never questioned it. I just did it. I didn't even know what that was exactly, except that I knew it was asking God to help a person or situation.

My mother would often send donations away to various Catholic devotionals with a list of intentions to be prayed for. The donation would go to the monastery or convent, where the monks or nuns would spend their days in prayer. Beautiful Holy Cards would come in the mail with pictures of Jesus or the Blessed Mother. Then we simply filled out the information and sent it to someone for their birthday or special occasion to let them know special prayers were being said for them. We had drawers full of these cards at the ready, to be sent at a moment's notice. *Okay*, I thought, *you can never have too many prayers, so that makes sense.*

That concept grew in me as I got older. When my mother became ill, after she had a miscarriage when I was in high school, I remember asking one of the sisters who taught me to pray for her. Somehow, if Sister Mary Carol prayed, her prayers would surely make a difference, more so than just mine would. She always promised to pray for me. There was great consolation in her words: "Don't worry, I will pray." I entered the convent after high school and made a personal promise that I would always pray for those who asked for my help. I wouldn't just promise to pray. I would really do it on the spot if I could.

As Sister Rosie, and even now, I was approached often to pray for various situations and illnesses. With never a thought, I attentively went about my task of asking God to be merciful and grant relief to whomever was ill, or to help so and so's dad find a job, or to console that family who had just lost a loved one and grant eternal rest to the one who had just died. I would simply unite my prayers and petitions with those who were asking, and together, we would approach God for help. That concept was not foreign to me. It was as natural as breathing.

Later in my life, someone challenged me, asking:

"Why do you pray for so and so? Let them ask themselves."

And, "Why do you pray to Saints for help? Are you afraid to talk directly to God?"

As an adult, it didn't seem good enough to just say, "I don't know. It's just something I grew up doing. I simply never thought about why!"

But was I afraid of approaching God myself?

Scripture is full of passages where we are encouraged to ask for what we need. In Matthew's Gospel, we are consoled by the words: "Come to me all you who are weary and find life burdensome and I will refresh you . . . " (11:28) or, in Luke's Gospel: "Ask and you will receive, seek and you will find, knock and the door will be opened" (11:9), and my personal favorite in Mark's Gospel is the story of Blind Bartimaeus. This story really illustrates the idea of interceding for another person. If I might set the scene for this, I am not going to read the passage. I am going to simply tell the story.

Here is this blind man, sitting on the side of the road just outside the town of Jericho. Jesus and his disciples were just leaving the town, and they had gathered a sizable crowd around them. This blind man, Bartimaeus, was waiting for who knows how long for Jesus to come by. Finally, he hears the crowd and knows Jesus is coming, and he begins to call out, "Jesus, son of David, have pity on me."

A pure request from the heart. But he's making a nuisance of himself, and the crowd is getting frustrated with him and telling him to be quiet. But Bartimaeus will have none of it and shouts all the louder, "Jesus, please have pity on me." His persistence pays off, and Jesus stops.

Now, I've been there on pilgrimage, and the streets are not that wide. It would have been easier for Jesus to walk over to him and see what the commotion was about. Instead, he says to the crowd around him, "Call him over," or in some translations, "Bring him to me."

The crowd surrounding Jesus wonders, *Uh oh, what's this? Jesus is paying attention to this nobody who is embarrassing us by yelling out for help!* But they go to him and say, "You have nothing to fear from him! Get up! He's calling you!"

It's almost as if you can hear Bartimaeus muttering under his breath, "Are you kidding? I'm not afraid. I've been here for days just waiting for this chance."

Scripture says that "immediately he threw off his cloak, jumped up, and came to Jesus." No hesitation. However, he needed assistance, since he was blind! They brought him to Jesus. And there he stood before Jesus, staring into space, unable to see. And Jesus asks him, "What do you want me to do for you?"

What? Was it not obvious?

Bartimaeus said, "Rabbi, I want to see."

Jesus said, "Be on your way. Your faith has healed you."

Scripture says that after Jesus healed him, "Immediately, he received his sight and started to follow him up the road."

I prayed this one passage for eight days straight. It was customary for us to end our work year with a retreat, to refresh our souls and re-create our spirits. I was making an eight-day retreat and trying to come to some resolutions in my young life. My director on the retreat asked me to pick a passage from the New Testament where Jesus was directly interacting with the people around him. I chose this passage in Mark's Gospel (10:46-52).

I sat in quiet contemplation on the side of the road with Bartimaeus for eight days until this passage opened up to me. It's important to understand that praying scripture is not the same as studying it. Praying a passage becomes personal. What is it saying to me now? Not what the scripture writers meant at the time, or what was going on politically at the time, or what the interpretation is of a particular word. No, praying scripture is more personal to the individual. It's important to ask, *how is God speaking to me through this particular passage?* Finally, I was able to put myself in Bartimaeus' place, and when Jesus asked him what he wanted, I answered for myself—*my needs at the time*. It was an "aha" moment.

Jesus said to me, "Rosie, what do you want me to do for you?"

With tears rolling down my face, I made my request, and I truly felt Jesus' arms around me.

I still pray that passage, and my requests are varied depending on my needs at the time. Sometimes, I ask for a friend: "Lord, help my friend get a job and be able to pay their rent."

Or, "Lord, help the people on our prayer lists in whatever way they need."

There are so many worldly needs, and I feel my prayers help.

Let me point out several things here. First, Bartimaeus was persistent, unwavering, and unyielding in his pursuit of Jesus's attention. Even in the face of a crowd that was averse to him, he shouted all the louder. Persistence in prayer is crucial. Keep asking, and don't be afraid to ask for what you need.

Sometimes, I just sit and feel very distant, not sure if I'm being heard. It might take all the energy I have to stay in prayer. I laugh when I say this, but sometimes all I can get out of my mouth is a helpless sound, much like, "Whaa? Huh? Uh?" But I stay there, patiently waiting for Jesus to come by.

Second, Jesus used the community, the crowd, to intercede for him. He could have simply walked a few steps over to Bartimaeus himself. Instead, he said, "Bring him to me." *As if he had said, "Hey, you guys who were telling him to be quiet, pick him up, and YOU bring him to me."* And this is my point: We need one another to help us when we can't move or see for ourselves. That is Intercessory Prayer. I know I can pray for what I need myself, but it gives me strength when I know others are praying with me and for me.

When I was young and still living at home, I would say to my friend, "You go ask mom if I can spend the night." I was not afraid of my mom, but I felt my chances were better if she asked, too. So together, we would approach my mom, all smiles with pleading looks, and ask for this favor. We received strength when we asked together.

Third, Jesus asked Bartimaeus to say what he needed, even though Jesus knew by looking at him. Yet Jesus asked specifically: "What do you want me to do for you?"

"Rabbi, I want to see."

Jesus' words to him—"Receive your sight, your faith has healed you"—are profound.

He didn't say, "Okay, hold on a minute. What makes you think you are worthy or good enough for this gift of sight?" He probably touched him gently, as there is healing in the act of touch, and told him it was his faith that made this happen.

And once healed, Bartimaeus didn't say, "Wow, how cool is this? Wait until I tell the gang." No, he put his gratitude into action and followed Jesus up the road. Then the people around him brought him to Jesus.

Many people ask me, "Rosie, please pray for me, or please pray for this intention."

It's as if they are saying, "Will you go with me to the Lord and stand with me as I ask for what I need? I can't do it alone. I am blind of heart or emotions, or my relationships are broken, and I am stuck in my pain."

My presence in their life at the time is like me saying, "You have nothing to fear. He's calling you. Go to him and ask, and I will go with you."

When we pray to saints, that is the intention: "St. Anthony, go with me to the Lord as I pray in supplication for my needs."

I have facilitated an intercessory prayer group for close to twenty-five years. Ten of us ladies meet monthly for prayer and updates. We started out meeting for prayer and discussion around various topics that I would prepare. Then, invariably, someone would ask for prayers for a family member or a friend. We started writing the requests down and updating each other on the progress of the one being prayed for. As our list grew, our time in prayer and in sharing got longer.

Eventually, our focus shifted from discussion topics to exclusively prayer on behalf of others. We get requests from all over now, as friends of friends have told others about us. We have experienced firsthand some miraculous outcomes. Our prayers may consist of praying for a happy death for an individual, or a job, or freedom from drug or alcohol addiction. Nothing is insignificant. We pray for any and all who come to us.

We use only first names and last initials to keep information confidential. We meet to enjoy lunch together or to watch a movie, and to simply allow the Holy Spirit to move among us. Years ago, we watched the film, *Divine Secrets of the Ya-Ya Sisterhood* (2002). We sort of adopted that name for ourselves. So now we get calls to ask the Ya-Ya's to pray!

We are great friends! We bring our own needs to the group as well, and together, we help discern God's call or offer advice through prayer. Our one-hour meeting turns into three hours sometimes. We meet at someone's home and have refreshments and lots of laughter and hugs. God's presence is truly felt, and we leave energized and ready to face whatever is in store for us!

Covid altered the home meetings for several years. When it let up, we started meeting at a restaurant for breakfast. What a ministry it has become. We have a few long-distance members who live in other states and affiliate with us as a support group.

Next time someone asks you to pray for them, and you say yes, think about the tremendous privilege it is for you to walk with that person to the Lord. And next time you ask for prayers, think about what you are requesting.

Ask them, "What do you want me to do for you?"

Powerful words! Don't be afraid to ask specifically. Asking for sight restoration is a big request, but hey, why not go for it? Nothing is unimportant. We may feel unworthy to ask, but we are encouraged to do so.

"Come to me if you are burdened and weary and find life difficult. I will refresh you." That invitation isn't qualified with "everyone but you can come." No, it is inclusive of all of us. And sometimes, we may need the support of friends to come with us in prayer as we ask. "Bring him or her to me."

Intercessory prayer is prayer on behalf of another. We can all do it. It only takes a moment, and miracles can happen when we do.

In the movie *Shadowlands* (1993), CS Lewis, played by Anthony Hopkins, is asked by a friend why he prays. And he answers that he prays because he is helpless, and that the need for prayer pours out of him around the clock, and that prayer transforms him.

Chapter Nineteen

There's more to you than the worst thing you've ever done.

Ihave lived an exciting life and have been blessed on many levels. The people and events that have been a part of my life have left an indelible mark on my heart and have helped form me into the person I am today.

Relating the many experiences that I have had, and sharing about the range of people that I have met throughout my 57 years of direct ministry, is a testament to how God has intervened in my life. Why do certain people come into our lives? I especially wonder this about people we would not seek out intentionally. There is one person in particular that I was led to quite by accident. I will keep his name confidential for obvious reasons.

I don't think it is any secret that the movie *Dead Man Walking* (1995) made a life-altering impression on me. Now, it may seem strange to hear me say that. It is an awe-inspiring, real-life portrayal of the unusual friendship that grew between a Catholic sister and a convicted murderer on death row. Sister Helen Prejean wrote the book first, and then the movie industry picked it up, and a film was made of her story.

She broke down walls and stereotypes that under-standably are raised and developed when we read of a crime, especially if that crime took the life of another. We fly into a rage and label the person who committed the crime as evil, and in our outrage, we want revenge. That is just part of how we express our feelings and deal with things that surpass our ability to make sense of them.

Destructive acts exasperate us, and some people want to lash out at the person responsible and make it right; this can mean leveling a similar punishment on the guilty person. I am not going to go into the pros and cons of the death penalty, especially with all that happens on a daily basis. I want to concentrate on the relationship that grew between Sister Helen and the convicted murderer, then insert my own personal experience.

This movie came out in 1995. Sister Helen is a Sister of St. Joseph, a branch of the same community that I was part of for 35 years. As a former Sister of St. Joseph, I felt an allegiance to her, and I went to see the movie with my friend Mary Ann. Throughout the movie, I remember going through a variety of emotions: from sorrow and outrage because of the crime, to pain and sadness for the family that experienced the loss, to anger toward the man for his refusal to take responsibility for his actions, and finally to frustration for Sister Helen for her valiant efforts to try and instill in him some redemptive qualities.

She was relentless in interceding on his behalf to the

appeals court to have his sentence commuted from death to life without parole. There were so many emotions that trudged heavily inside of me throughout this movie. I was exhausted when it was over. My friend and I sat in stone silence while the credits played and the theater emptied. Finally, we were the last to leave, while the broom brigade marched in to clean things up. While walking to our car, I uttered these fateful words:

"I don't know about you, but I could never do what she did. No way."

Ah, I should know better by now, never to give God any leverage over me. Less than two weeks later, I received a call from a colleague who was the Director of Detention Ministry for the Seattle Archdiocese. Michael was responsible for the spiritual support of inmates in the prisons in Western Washington. She said there was a man up in my area who was on trial for murder, and that he was asking for a spiritual person to talk to. She said she didn't have a chaplain that far north to visit this man, and she wondered if I would be willing to take this on.

Before I made the decision, she wanted to meet with me to give me some newspaper clippings about him and his particular case. She wanted to brief me a little more about what my role would be and the necessary steps I would have to take before I actually met him. And further, she would have to put me in contact with his lawyers, who would then set up the actual meeting. In addition, I would have to go through a screening process before I would be considered for this assignment.

"So please come in," she said, "and I will give you his file and answer any questions you may have."

I ran this by Sister Suzanne, who worked in the Detention Ministry for most of her religious life. She understood my concerns, but she encouraged me to give his lawyers a call.

I hung up the phone, and a cold sweat came over me. "You have got to be kidding me," I exclaimed. "This can't be real!"

It took a few days before I traveled the 60+ miles down to Seattle. When my friend came into the room, she had a smirk on her face as if to say, "I am so sorry to do this to you." She knew I was in transition from my community, and that I was in the midst of making a life-changing decision about my future in ministry. She handed me a file with information about this man and his alleged crime. In the file were newspaper clippings of him and his story. I remember thinking that he didn't look like a hardened criminal; he appeared more frightened than anything.

She also handed me a small Post-it note with his lawyer's' phone number. "Think and pray about this and give them a call," she said. "They'll tell you what to do next." This was like the film, *Mission Impossible!*

I drove home totally numb and kind of sick to my stomach. Scenes from that movie kept playing out over and over in my mind. I prayed, "Dear Lord, please no . . . not this! Please don't ask this of me!"

I went home and kind of halfheartedly skimmed the contents of the file folder, then left it on my desk. "Not tonight. Tomorrow, maybe!"

I stuck the Post-it note on the screen of my computer and closed the door, and I didn't look at it for several days. I was secretly hoping that his lawyers had come up with an alternative, since it had been weeks since they made their initial request. Finally, feeling guilty, I couldn't hold back any longer, and I called them, fully expecting them to say, "Thanks anyway, but we found someone else close by."

Instead, I was greeted with, "Thanks for getting back to us. We've been expecting your call."

Oh, no! I fumbled around, trying to find my voice, so I could sound like I was glad they had waited for me. My heart was pounding, and I felt weak. I pulled it together and made an appointment to drive up in a day or two and meet them. I figured I needed a little time to compose myself and pray this through.

On my way up the interstate, I had a sinking feeling that this was going to be a Kairos moment. Kairos is a Greek word meaning a moment in time when our lives intersect the ever-present love of God, unplanned, but precisely at the moment when we need it most. This was such a moment! I couldn't explain it, but I knew it would be another life-altering experience. I mean, if it were anything like the movie, I was in for an intense awakening.

I was met with great enthusiasm and prepared with all I should know prior to actually meeting with their client. They gave me more information about his life and the circumstances that had brought him into the system. They told me I had to go over to the jail, to get some forms to fill out and to see about the screening process that was necessary before I could see him. The screening process consisted of a background check and some references. I had no idea. It took weeks before I was actually seated face-to-face with him.

It really was as gray and stark as prisons are portrayed in the movies. Only this wasn't a penitentiary. It was a county jail with maximum security. They had me drop my purse, driver's license, and car keys in a drawer, much like at the teller's window at a bank. They kept everything while I was with him. They directed me through heavy metal doors to a small, closet-like room that had a chair and a phone receiver attached to the wall. Thick bulletproof glass separated me from the person on the other side. The room had no ventilation or windows of any kind. I had a doorknob inside my room to let me out, but he did not. A guard escorted him in. I walked in freely.

And there I was, seated across from this slightly built man who didn't resemble his pictures at all. The photos in the newspapers almost always pictured him with a smirk, or a frown, or a non-caring look, or even appearing to be in conflict with his lawyers.

He was written up as arrogant, unremorseful, and even dangerous. So, I was ready. I was going to hold my own against him. I would not let him intimidate me. However, he was not in any way the person he was portrayed to be. We had to talk via the phone on the wall. His handcuffs were taken off so he could reach the receiver and push the button to talk. My phone kept shorting out, and I had to hold it in just the right way for the connection to work, or it would go dead. We talked for close to two hours, and he shared with me like he had known me all his life. By then, my head was splitting from lack of air and stress. I told him we needed to bring our time to a close. He looked sad and said, "I bet you don't come back. None of them ever do."

This monster that I had anticipated meeting had suddenly turned into a person with a history and a family. He had a slight stammer in his speech, but when he got going and knew I was listening, he could talk without stammering. When I said I had to go, his stutter came back. I assured him that I would return, and he put his hand up to the window, and I placed mine up to touch his, and we said goodbye. I walked out of the small room on my own while he sat and waited for a guard to come and get him.

When I went to pick up my personal items, I asked the guard if there was another place where I could meet him instead of those small telephone booth-type rooms. No air and the phones don't work well. He said he'd look into it for me by the time I came back next week.

"You are coming back next week, aren't you?" he asked.

"Yes, I am coming back next week."

By the time I returned the following week, they had received a final letter of recommendation from the archbishop's office. Well, I don't have to tell you I was treated differently. The staff was all smiles asking, "How was your day so far," and saying, "Come this way."

They took me beyond security, through two sets of heavy slamming doors, down a hallway with occupied cells on either side. Inmates peeked out through the small slits in the doors where their food is pushed through. I was taken to a room with a table and bench on either side, much like at a fast-food place where the heavy Formica benches are part of the table. He was brought down the hall by a guard. No handcuffs. He sat across the table from me, two feet away. The guard left us alone and went back to his post at the end of the hall.

I was not given a time limit; I could stay as long as I wanted. They would bring his dinner to him if we went into dinner time! A far cry from last week's visit! That was where we met every Thursday for more than six months. I heard his life story, and eventually, he got around to talking about the incident that put him in jail. I never pressured him. I just sat and listened. We laughed and were silent together many times during those months.

When he did give an account of the details of the crime, I sat very quietly, not wanting to show any signs of judgment through my facial expressions or body language. And because of this, he kept right on talking. His candid sharing was difficult to hear. He finally started to show some emotion, and I reached across the table and touched him. He did not pull away. By that time, I was emotional, too.

I said a simple prayer, asking God to cleanse him from the terrible crime that now sat in his heart. He expressed remorse and asked for God's forgiveness and mine. Mine? Why mine? He had come to respect me and care for me as his friend. He was embarrassed by what he had done. He felt that perhaps I would leave him now that I knew.

The man across from me was no longer a killer, but

a person with a history, a mother, brother, sisters, and a child. All of them had turned their backs on him and told the state to go ahead and kill him! He knew what he had done was wrong, but after listening to all that led up to it, I saw things in a different light than what I had read in the newspapers. I couldn't change the outcome or tell him he wasn't at fault. I could only offer my friendship and stand by him for support in the weeks to come.

His trial ended, and he was convicted of aggravated first-degree murder. The sentence would be either life without parole or death by lethal injection. The day before his sentencing, his lawyers called me. They were frantic, asking me to come and talk to him, as he was becoming anxious in his cell from the stress and anticipation. They were afraid that he would make a scene in the courtroom when it was time for him to be sentenced.

I went and met with him and tried to calm him down. I made him promise that when the judge asked if he had anything to say, he wouldn't go off on him. I told him that if I felt him getting agitated, I would cough, and that would be his signal to calm down. I showed up at the courthouse, went into his courtroom, and sat down close to where he and his lawyers were. The family of the victim filed in and sat next to me. They were given a chance to read a victim impact statement in which they called him all sorts of names with hatred and anger in their voices. He sat there, hands cuffed tightly to his side with chains and locks. His feet were chained together as well. I remember thinking how odd that felt to see him bound up, after we had sat together for months with no restraints at all, and I was never afraid.

Finally, after all the statements were read, the judge asked him to stand, and I could see by his breathing that he was stressed. He didn't have anything to say on his behalf, and he just asked the judge to proceed. I gave a little cough and cleared my throat, and his shoulders relaxed. I sat, staring into the judge's face as my friend was sentenced to death by lethal injection.

His head dropped to his chest. I stopped breathing for what seemed like an eternity. His lawyers shot a glance over to me. Tears welled up in my eyes, and I lost all sense of time and what happened next. I only remember that two guards took him by the arms, one on each side, and marched him past me. I looked right at him and hoped that my eyes would say it all. I could not reach out to touch him, yet just the day before, he gave me a hug and thanked me for standing by him. We hugged each other after our sessions each week, and he told me that meant a lot to him because he knew that I was not afraid of him. He was not a serial killer. The crime had occurred during a moment in time when he had lost all control out of rage and did a terrible thing.

I let him go, and within a few days, he was transferred to the state penitentiary east of the mountains. I have not seen him since, but we write, and there have been the occasional phone calls. Life on death row is another story for another time. I care for this man and promise to be with him when the time comes. At present, we are trying to have his sentence commuted to life without parole.

There are circumstances that warrant that request.

Why do I tell this story? For many reasons. Again, the reminder that there is more to a person than the worst thing they've ever done. We just don't know the whole story behind what we read in the papers or see on TV. There are consequences to our actions, and we will have to deal with those consequences. Once an action is completed, we cannot take it back. Words kill, as well as guns and knives. "Thou shalt not kill" refers to all forms of defamation. We can kill a reputation with our words of envy or hatred. Gossip kills friendships and breaks down trust.

I had this man tried and convicted in my mind before I ever met him. And this was based on his pictures and the things written about him in the newspaper by people who probably never even talked to him or interviewed him. I met a human being, and I spent time letting him know that God had not turned his back on him, and neither would I.

He had no family support. He was alone. And now, in his six-by-nine-foot cell, he was interacting with no one, twenty-four hours a day. He had one hour a day to walk around an empty basketball court for minimal exercise. He showered with a guard within feet of him. All forms of dignity were taken away because of one moment in time. He made a mistake and is now paying the supreme price. But I am his friend and his link to the outside world, and I will be with him if that last day ever happens. To me, that is the gospel message.

Life is full of twists and turns in the road. We are responsible for how we travel that road, but there is more to us than the worst thing we've ever done. He brought that home to me in a dramatic way. I continue to write him and talk to his lawyers when permitted. His letters are simple and heartfelt. He is not making excuses for what he did. He is grateful that I did not turn my back on him, but that I stayed with him through it all.

Because of him, I am much slower to judge and condemn. As hard as this was, it was one of the most worthwhile experiences of my life. There is not one of us who doesn't have something in our past that we are ashamed of—something we wish we had never done or said. Psychologists claim that we subconsciously hate in others the weaknesses we most despise in ourselves. This man's indiscretion was all over the media. Ours is hidden and unknown, perhaps only to ourselves.

In John's Gospel, some teachers of the law brought a woman to Jesus who had been caught in the act of adultery. They were trying to trip him up and said, "The law says that we are to stone people like her. What do you say?"

Jesus bent down and started writing in the sand. Then he straightened up and asked them, "Are any of you without sin? Then, you cast the first stone."

One by one, they began to leave, beginning with the eldest. Some believe Jesus was writing the sins of those who were condemning her.

Jesus said to her, "Has no one condemned you?"

"No one, sir," she said.

"Then, neither do I. Go and don't sin anymore."

That is gospel compassion and forgiveness. I couldn't

take his crime away, but I could offer him gospel compassion and forgiveness. In the light of all the executions that are becoming too common again, my firsthand experience with this man further validates what I have come to believe: Jesus was above reproach and criticism in a way none of us could ever be, and yet, he showed only compassion. Not condoning the behavior, but never rejecting the person. Not easy to do, but I invite you to sit with that concept for a while and see where your heart leads you.

Footnote: Since this interview, our governor has abolished the death penalty. My friend was next in line, but now he is no longer on death row; he is instead serving a sentence of life without parole. His lawyers interceded on his behalf, and the many letters that I shared with them, showing his remorse, I would like to think helped in achieving this new sentence, along with my prayers and advocacy. We remain friends and continue to write. Our exchanges are much more relaxed now, since greeting cards are acceptable. I can share pictures and holy cards as well.

He gave me a heartfelt compliment in one of his letters, saying, "If I had met you years ago, this never would have happened."

All in God's time.

Chapter Twenty

Spiritual Direction

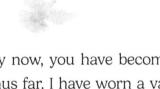

I'm guessing that by now, you have become aware that over my lifetime, thus far, I have worn a variety of hats! It has been fun reminiscing on how those hats came about. One in particular has been a blessing over the years—my hat as spiritual director. Earlier, I shared how, as a young sister, I had been trained and certified for this ministry. Now, many years later, I am well experienced and know that this hat has been well worn, and that the stories about it are many.

I think it is safe to say that many people are not sure what spiritual director actually means. The majority of people that I interact with have a private internal sense of God in their lives but want to enhance that closeness. And so, spiritual direction is nothing more than a conversation between two people, in which one person counsels the other about how God may be touching their life, either directly or indirectly. Sometimes this is called "spiritual companionship." Simply put, spiritual direction is helping people tell their sacred stories.

Jesus counseled his chosen. For three years, they experienced direct spiritual guidance from him. The Beatitudes in Matthew's Gospel are profound insights into God's benevolence. God is so integral to our day-to-day lives, gently moving us to do good, to make decisions, and to share with others. I see people who want to nurture their prayer life or develop one, or to share with me how they feel God is acting in their lives. Some have sustained a loss of a job, friendship, or health, or perhaps they have suffered through the death of a loved one. And they wonder where God is in all that pain. Or they may be discerning a change in their life and want to talk about what it means.

A spiritual director listens, travels with the person down their road, and helps them deal with grief, or with those dry periods that come with prayer. When I was considering leaving my religious community after 35 years, I sought the guidance of a professional counselor, as well as my spiritual director. The counselor helped me deal with some issues that were standing in the way of making a good decision. And my spiritual director helped me find God and peace in my decision.

I know that God is found at our peace level. That has been my experience. When I finally made the decision to leave the community with the help of my spiritual director, I had a consuming sense of peace. I had no money and no job, but I knew it was right. I was at peace and knew my decision would be blessed.

A wonderful part of my ministry is being part of another person's search for God. Or helping a person heal after a loss. Or seeing the look of contentment when they experience an "aha" moment and know God is there. It is gratifying. And if I feel that an individual is in need of professional counseling, even though I am licensed and qualified to help them, I refer them to someone who can help them on another level. I don't want to get my role confused with their other issues, even though they may overlap. I know the difference, and I am not afraid to say that I think they need some more direct counseling beyond what I can offer them.

My clients were varied. They consisted of housewives, professionals, and anyone who wanted to improve their prayer life and find ways to deepen their communication with God. Sometimes, these encounters were monthly, while others had only one or two visits just to talk. Sometimes, colleagues would ask to talk to me so they could share an experience they had with a patient and ask me for advice. I had a client who is a deacon in his church and shared his spiritual reading with me. Dennis was a friend, and our time usually entailed talking about upcoming events in our lives or how the family was doing. It was informal but prayerful. Our discussions were rich, challenging, and a means of growth for both of us.

Life is a challenge, and sometimes, we are so closely intertwined with the challenges of life that we can't see the hand of God in it. As I've shared, another person listening may be able to point out possibilities and highlight areas of growth that we might not otherwise see ourselves, to help us come to an unbiased resolution. Another set of ears can hear things we can't. Often, we have the answers, and we just need some help to access them.

As a hospice chaplain, I was often in a spiritual direction situation as patients poured their hearts out in an effort to touch the hand of God. There may be a scripture passage that might support the conversation and help the person to pray. Like that passage I spoke about earlier, that I prayed for eight days straight. Finally, I heard Jesus ask me, "Rosie, what do you want me to do for you?"

Spiritual directors are nothing more than companions on the way. Jesus sent his disciples out two by two to be spiritual support for one another. I guess my ministry over the years has been geared toward bringing harmony and peace to the individual.

God's love is unconditional. It is not earned. It is freely given no matter what. In the end, we will not have to submit our baptismal certificate. There is a saying that's been around for some time:

"Our life is God's gift to us. What we make of our life is our gift to God."

Whatever our particular faith expression has been, whatever spiritual road God has led us down, walk that road with purity of intention and integrity of heart. Seek counsel to walk it better if you need to. We don't all have to be on the same road, just going in the same direction.

And when our time is nearing completion, look back and see the legacy you've left behind. What did you do with what you were given? Did you love enough?

Love like you've never loved before. Accept love like

you've never accepted anything before. And give with no strings attached. Choose life every chance you get. Let your life be a testament to God's love. Leave this world better than when you entered it. Laugh, cry, rejoice, and be a blessing. Learn from others and share your blessings with others. Enter into another person's world just for a moment to see how they see life.

I wrote a small twenty-seven-page book on football: *Football Doesn't Have to Be a Dirty Word, A Woman's Guide to Understanding the Sport.*

It's hardly a treatise, but I've been on TV five times because of it and interviewed over the radio more times than I can count. I wrote it for women mostly. Why? If you love the person who loves the sport, then learn a little bit so you can share the experience with them. I believe stepping over into another person's comfort zone enhances the relationship. It may not be your comfort zone, but every now and then, you've got to cross over that line.

The small book is easy to read in thirty minutes or less. It gives just enough insight so that you at least know what's going on. Some hardcore football enthusiasts have found fault with some of my explanations, but they work. The book is told from my perspective. Not from the perspective of the commissioner of football. It has helped a lot of women, who are otherwise miserable during football season when their partners are consumed by watching games. It can be great fun if you know just enough. Then, the rest begins to make sense, because you have a baseline from which to ask your next question.

My dad played semi-pro ball, and when we would watch a game together, I would ask a lot of questions. He patiently helped me understand just enough. The rest I picked up by watching. Things begin to hook together, and before you know it, you've got a fundamental grasp of the game. And the popcorn tastes better when you happily watch the game together. If I see the need while in a spiritual direction session, I freely give a copy of the book to bridge the gap and bring about peace. Works like a charm!

Chapter Twenty-One

When that light turns green,
my life is going to change!

Well, if you've made it this far in the book, you see how my life has indeed been led by the Spirit. I mean, the words "been there, done that" have taken on new meaning. Unless I live to be 130, I am way past middle age, and I was looking forward to the final chapters in this interesting life of mine.

"What next, Lord?" I should know better than to ask.

After I became free from my vows and was a lay-woman, that concept was foreign to me. I had left home at seventeen and at the time was in my fifties. I thought that I should be ready for some much-needed downtime. However, while counseling a couple prior to their wedding, they shared with me that they met online. I had heard of the phenomenon, but it didn't concern me. Not at this age. I was content to be just "Rosie" and enjoy my independence. However, I was intrigued by what they had shared. So, as I often do, I put a test strip down before God to see if anyone is listening.

"If I am supposed to explore this concept," I prayed, "please have a free trial show up in my emails."

The next day, while surfing through my many emails and eliminating a bunch, I saw in bold print a free invitation to place my profile information on a website, to see if there was anyone out there interested in meeting me! Cupid Junction, no less!

"Oh, come on, I was just kidding!"

But just for fun, I wrote up my profile, being very honest about what I was and wasn't looking for. I gave the age requirements and said I hoped the person had a sense of humor and some education. It was supposed to be safe in that they would have no way of contacting me except through the Junction. I sent it off with a picture. I was not looking for marriage, just companionship.

Within the hour, I received more than 200 profiles of men who might be what I was looking for. I scrolled through the names and pictures and was totally discouraged. The pickin's were slim! Who was I kidding, at my age, in my mid-fifties? There was not much out there to catch my eye. Then, as I was almost ready to shut down the search, there he was! No pretense. A simple headshot, a sweet smile, and he had hair! He was handsome, and we were 93% compatible.

I decided to save his profile, so I wouldn't have to scroll down trying to find him. Unbeknownst to me, my saving actually shot my profile to him. He replied! I could hear the Holy Spirit's wings flapping in the breeze!

"Would you like to meet?" he asked.

I was numb! I didn't answer for a day. He tried again. No response from me. What had I started? Finally, he said he would leave me alone if I wasn't interested. I responded. We met for lunch several days later at a lovely restaurant midway from each other. He lived a little over an hour from me!

Getting off the freeway, I said to myself, "When this light turns green, my life is going to change."

There he was, sitting on a bench inside, waiting for me. We introduced ourselves and were seated at our booth. We talked for hours. At one point, his sister called to see what he was up to.

"I'm sitting with the woman I'm going to marry," he told her.

In your dreams, buddy!

Now that should have been the deal breaker! It wasn't. I had said in my profile that I had an interesting background that would be a good conversation piece. As we talked, he realized I had never been married. I was a career woman most of my life, and I was well-educated. He said I intrigued him and wanted to know, "Who are you?"

Finally, he asked about my interesting background. Teasingly, I said to a drum roll, "I was a hooker!" I couldn't believe those words slipped out of my mouth!

His look said it all! I broke out laughing. He didn't know what to say or do.

I said, "What would be the exact opposite of hooker?"

He came up with nothing!

Again, to a drum roll, I said very slowly and dramatically, "For over 35 years, I was a Roman Catholic Nun!"

Again, the look! Only this time, it was one of relief!

It all began to make sense to him. There I sat with minimal makeup, in a simple skirt and blouse, hardly the outfit of a hooker. He asked more questions. I was totally honest in my responses. It was a comfortable conversation. I am proud of my family and shared with him about my parents, my sisters, and my brother. I told him Cheech was my cousin, and that extended our conversation at least another hour.

He told me about his family. Five children, and at that time, 14 grandchildren. We had a good meal, and the hours went by quickly. He walked me to my car and asked if he could kiss me. He did before I could answer. That should have been strike two! But it wasn't! We met again several weeks later at a little Mexican restaurant. And kissed in the parking lot in the rain.

I was overwhelmed and confused. This was uncharted territory to me. I hadn't been kissed since high school, years ago.

"Where is this going? Dear Lord, help me!"

Finally, I invited him to my home. He played his trumpet, and I played my guitar. I was feeling something. But what? We'd been dating for several months. Our dates consisted of him accompanying me to weddings I was officiating. Perfect. We could dress up and have a wonderful meal. He was proud of my ministry and made friends easily at the receptions. One day, he told me he was going to Kuwait to work for the military. He wanted to dissolve all of his debts and enter into this relationship debt-free. This would be an eighteen-month commitment.

In a way, I was relieved! Things were moving too fast. I needed to collect my thoughts. He needed to be out of the picture for me to do that. After he left, I missed him. We talked on the phone when we could, and he came home every few months for two weeks. The following January, on his leave home, he proposed to me.

"Yes!" I shocked myself! I called my mom to tell her I was engaged. I had kept my parents up to date on our relationship, so this was not an "out of the blue" announcement.

My sweet mamma said, "Oh Mija, we haven't had the mother-daughter talk yet!"

We both laughed, and I loved her for those words. She would tell my dad, and I would call my sisters! This relationship was never what I would ever have envisioned for my life!

On home leave in July, Ron met my immediate family. He emotionally asked my parents for my hand in marriage. He teared up, and so did I. My sisters prepared a lovely luncheon on the veranda in Pat's beautiful backyard. Then, a few days later, on July Fourth, my parents' anniversary, he met my extended family. We had a huge celebration for Mom and Dad and then a surprise wedding shower for us. He was immediately one of the family! I was bursting with pride as the family I had grown to respect and love welcomed us as a couple. It was pleasantly overwhelming.

On Thanksgiving Day in 2005, we were married in a beautiful ceremony around the pool at my parents' home, with my friend Father Thomas Allsopp officiating! Gary and Katie Dahlstadt, who had become our best friends, drove from Mount Vernon, Washington, to Woodland Hills, California, with our clothes, so they wouldn't get wrinkled in a suitcase on the flight. Gary could be Ron's best man, and Katie could read from the Book of Ruth, "Wherever you go, I will go . . . " With 100 friends and family present, including members of my former community, we said, "I do!"

Ron was so handsome, and my sisters did my hair and some light makeup. Mom and Dad blessed me, and they walked me in to a resounding applause. My sisters, again, made the day memorable with beautiful decorations, something breathtaking at every turn. The reception was exceptional and complete with butlers. It was a reception filled with love. God provided the blue sky and perfect weather with ambiance galore. Strains of "That's Amore" filled the air and was the beginning of yet another new chapter in my life at sixty years of age.

"Come, Holy Spirit."

Chapter Twenty-Two

*God knew from all eternity that I would
care for my parents at the end of their lives.*

As you can imagine, adjusting to married life had its conditions. He had been single for twenty years, and I had never been married. We were set in our ways. He calls himself "Mr. Sister" and would remind me when "Mother Superior" would show up every now and then. I was still with hospice, and he was a Medicare broker. We worked hard to save money and pay our bills. I continued to be on call with the funeral homes in our valley. We were adjusting, both to one another and to a new way of life.

The years flew by, and my parents and sisters would come to visit around the Fourth of July, for their anniversary celebration with my friends here in the valley. We'd go down to LA for Christmas. We made it work. We moved to a larger home so we could each have an office.

Just before the move, and while my parents were visiting with Pat after Christmas, we received a phone call that my brother had suffered a fatal heart attack. Our visit was cut short, and the four of us flew to my folks' home to prepare for his service and console one another and his daughter Midori.

My brother was an amazing man full of talent. His internal struggles got the best of him, and he passed peacefully while Mom, Dad, and Pat were with us. We celebrated his life at Mass with prayer, music, and stories. We have many Louie stories, and they come up in conversation often. We leaned on one another through it all. It was hard to believe that he was gone. Our big brother. He was too young. My parents forever grieved because of it. Grief has a way of taking on a life of its own. Since our wedding, we have lost many guests. Among them were Jooj's husband, George, whom I loved and whose funeral service I officiated. My heart still misses him. The frailness of life continued to hit us in the heart. You would think that my years with hospice would have prepared me for all the losses.

Then, Mom and Dad came to live with us. They were in their mid to late nineties. A series of circumstances made it apparent that our home was the best place for them to be. My sister Pat had Mom and Dad for seven years after we closed down their home. Then they lived with my mom's two sisters, Elsa and Grace, who were up in age, and the living situation was not good for any of them.

So, sadly, we had to close "Casa Woody," as we fondly referred to it. They lived in Woodland Hills. Cheech had provided that home for them for more than 35 years. My aunt Elsa lived with her daughter Orbie (Elena). Aunt Grace lived with my cousin Maggie. Mom and Dad went to live with Pat. It was a difficult transition for everyone, as Casa Woody was the family home for all of us cousins.

The hope was that they would live with Pat for six months, and then with me for six months once she moved to South Carolina to be close to her daughter and grandchildren. It didn't take long before we realized that Mom and Dad were too frail to travel.

Dad had been showing signs of dementia, and Mom followed shortly after. Ron, being a Medicare broker, immediately got them a good insurance policy, and luckily we lived near the hospital and various doctors. I found a doctor willing to assume care for my elderly parents. She was kind and patient with their memory lapses. The move was hard on them, as they had never lived outside of Los Angeles. My friends took to them like they were their own, as did Ron, and they began to see our house as their home.

It was hard to see them decline. They had always been vibrant and full of life. My sisters would come as often as they could to visit and give me and Ron a break. They added a fun dimension to the days. And they were great cooks who were always ready for a happy hour with hors d'oeuvres and all.

Even though I had cared for hospice patients for many years, I was not mentally prepared for this. I could leave a patient after a visit and go home. Now, these were my parents who needed my attention 24/7. I was not always the consoling chaplain like I was at work. It was like my brain turned off, and I was totally incompetent. These were my parents. I loved them and watched them decline in front of my eyes. And this is where the Spirit made itself known. That man who wandered into my life and took me by surprise became my rock and my strength. God knew from all eternity that I would be faced with the task of caring for my parents at the end of their lives. I needed the right support to do this. Ron was that support.

All the rules of how to talk to a person with dementia were buried in the back of my mind somewhere. I did well at chaplain visits, but with my parents, I was clueless. I was in a fog. Mostly because I was frightened to observe their decline. I had to pull it together.

Ron was great with Dad. He would take him on long rides to places Dad flew over while in the service. They would stop for lunch and ice cream. They would talk for hours. Dad loved Ron like a son, and they became best friends. When Dad had to have his pacemaker replaced, the doctors allowed Ron to get into scrubs and be with him during the procedure, as they could only give him a local. Ron held his hand the entire hour while Dad kept his eyes on him.

Ron was always looking for fun things that Dad would enjoy. One day, he discovered that a B-24 vintage WWII airplane was coming to town. Dad had been a radio operator on the B-24 during the war. Ron somehow talked his way into getting Dad and himself on the plane and flew to Seattle for free. When it was announced that Dad had been a radio operator on the B-24, the crowd that had assembled to see the plane let out a cheer as Ron and Dad made their way to the plane. My mom watched through teary eyes. They sat in the radio operator's seat. Their love and respect for one another was a gift.

Mom and I had our monthly hair appointments followed by lunch somewhere different each time. Mom loved the casino, and we would make our way there and sit and play penny slot machines for hours. I'd get snacks, and we'd eat while we played. One day, as we were driving out of town toward the casino, Mom said to me, "Mija, just this morning, I asked the Blessed Mother to put me on the right road that I am supposed to be on."

I listened for her answer.

After a short pause, she said, "And honey . . . this is the road!"

We both busted up laughing.

I often had to remind myself of those times when frustration or exhaustion would overtake me. I would check on them before I went to bed to be sure they were tucked in well. With a cross and a beep! They had their own bedroom and bathroom, but I slept with one ear cocked to hear any unforeseen noise that might mean a fall or a call for help. One night, I was pulling an all-nighter to get taxes done, when Ron came into my office at 4 AM to say that Mom and Dad were sitting in the front room fully dressed. They were confused and thought it was daytime. We had to convince them by pulling up the blinds that it was still dark. We marched them down the hall, muttering to themselves as they crawled back in bed. A sweet memory now!

My task was to make them feel as comfortable and loved as possible. I would make them their favorite food and snacks. Ice cream with a cookie was a must at night. At the beginning of their stay, when they were able, they would take a short stroll down our property for some exercise, holding hands. A sight I will never forget. They had been married for nearly eighty years. They met when they were young and were always together. Mom would poke Dad with her cane to get his attention, just to say she loved him. He would respond with, "I adore you." Their deep love for one another was our greatest gift from them.

Eventually, they were no longer able to be without constant supervision. Hospice was called in. It was time for some hands-on support. By this time, after more than four years of caring for them, I knew I could no longer do it alone. I was often close to tears because I knew they were on their final decline, and I would be with them when they passed.

Hospice was everything I knew it to be. The hospice nurses taught me about my parents' medications, and I set up a clinic in my office with a time sheet that helped me remember when to administer their medications. Ron and I could no longer monitor their showers. They were reluctant to have anyone come in to shower them, but it had to be done. I was worried when I had to tell them that someone was going to come to help them shower. As expected, they both said, "No way," and that they could do it themselves.

Two fine CNAs (certified nursing assistants) were assigned to us.

"Here we go," I thought, "Dad's guy comes today."

Luckily, we got a male bath aid for Dad. Both Mom and Dad were extremely modest, so it had to be the right person for them. What I wasn't prepared for was Ozz! I saw this large young man with his hair pulled back into a bun and a bandanna on his head. Plus, he had a beard and tattoos.

"Oh no, this will not end well."

I motioned to him at the window to come around to the back door. I needed to prepare him for Dad.

My dad was sitting in his recliner with his bathrobe on as he knew it was shower day. Then, Ozz followed me into the front room so I could introduce him to Dad. I crossed my fingers, not knowing how this would go. Both Mom and Dad just stared at this huge man before them. Ozz pulled up a small ottoman and sat down in front of Dad.

"Hi, Buddy," he said.

Dad smiled back, and then they began to chat. Dad is easy to talk to, and he took well to Ozz's relaxed and soft-spoken demeanor. I left and went into my office. Mom was speechless. Before long, the two of them were coming down the hall to the shower, laughing and talking like old friends. Hallelujah, one down!

A few days later, Kailynn arrived for Mom. A lovely young woman with a sweet smile. Mom knew she couldn't get out of this, so she and Kailynn made their way to the shower together. Both Mom and Dad had a walker by this time. After her shower, I asked Mom how it went.

With a big smile, she said, "Good. She really knows what she's doing!"

Kailynn did Mom's nails and dressed her in the clean clothes I had provided. A friendship was born. I was so grateful for this intervention, as I had been worried for weeks beforehand. The Holy Spirit was on call!

Their hospice team became my confidants. I could share my concerns and anxiety with them, and they understood. I received good advice, and I felt my burden lessen daily. My sisters came when they could. Ron was ever at my side. God knew I needed this man. He gave up his semi-retirement to care for my parents. I couldn't have asked for more.

As Dad became more frail, it was necessary for him to be in a hospital bed, in the front room where he used to sit and look out a huge window at the birds and squirrels and occasional rabbits. Mom was parked in her recliner next to him. Dad was now sleeping more, and Mom would say, "He looks peaceful, doesn't he?"

Dad passed peacefully with all of us with him. Mom heard us talking and wanted to know what had happened.

"Dad just went to heaven," I told her.

Mom melted into sobs. Her soul mate of 79 years was gone. It was hard to console her when we were completely devastated ourselves.

Dad had passed at 10:20 in the evening. We kept him all the next day and had a vigil prayer for him while we blessed him and anointed him with holy water. When Kern Funeral Home came for him, they draped him in the American flag, and Ron saluted him as they drove off. His buddy was gone.

A week later, we had a memorial service at our home. We invited his hospice team and friends who had grown to love him. Pat made a beautiful memorial program to give to everyone present, filled with his pictures and the prayers we were to say together. I put together a short ritual, and we all broke bread together and had refreshments while looking at a video of their life.

As long as Dad was by her side, Mom had the will to live. Without him now, she declined more rapidly. I found a way to engage Mom in prayer, and we would say the Rosary together with special family intentions. We talked about Dad often. She would sit and talk to him throughout the day.

"Who are you talking to?" I would ask her.

And she would say, "Dad."

"What is he saying to you?"

She said, "Not to worry. That I would be with him soon."

Mom slept in her recliner in the front room after Dad passed. She couldn't be in the bed without him. I slept on the couch next to her. She was without the man she had loved since she was 15. She could barely stand to be without him. It was hard to see her grieve so deeply. Then, one morning, she could not get out of her recliner to use the restroom.

I brought the commode into the living room for her. I couldn't transfer her, as she had no strength in her legs. I called hospice, and Mom was placed in the hospital bed. She searched my face for understanding. I think she knew that was the end for her in some way.

My sisters had just left a week before, and I called and said, "Come back. Mom's not doing well." They came immediately. Mom smiled when she saw them and then peacefully drifted off to sleep.

The three of us sat, touching her so she would know we were there. We prayed the Rosary and other prayers and told her we loved her until well into the morning. At 3 AM, we went to bed in the front room to be near her. Mom passed peacefully at 10:20 AM, six months after Dad. We were now alone without the people who had given us life. It was a hollow feeling. We kept Mom as we did Dad until the next evening. Then, a week later, we had a similar memorial service at the house for her hospice team and our friends.

This four-and-a-half-year journey was over. The two most important people in our lives were gone. I always thought they'd be with us forever. They were ready, as all of their family and friends were gone. My dad's youngest sister, Auntie Lu, survives them as part of the greatest generation, with its big band music that we used to play when we were all together. We'd drive down the road to someplace for dinner or for a week away, and Pat would play all the songs we knew by heart— Eydie Gorme, Los Panchos, and Frank Sinatra—and we would all sing along. We were loved and secure in that love all our lives.

Hospice was our support and strength. Competent nurses were available 24/7, along with social workers and bath aids. A volunteer, Missy, came weekly to visit with Mom and watch "Gunsmoke" on TV with her. A massage therapist came and relieved some stress in her back and legs. I relied on them to help me through the hardest ministry of my life. They didn't disappoint me. I was a part of the team for 13 years, but now, I completely appreciated the compassion and professional skills they brought to our home. Mom and Dad were well-cared for, and Ron and I and Jooj and Pat were able to give over the hands-on ministry so we could be their children and love them into eternity.

Jooj and I flew with Pat to her home in South Carolina for three weeks. We spent time with her daughter and son-in-law, Gia and Danny, and grandchildren, Peanut (Ava) and Declan. Jooj's son, Doug, joined us for the last week. This was our immediate family now. Those three weeks were special and sacred. We laughed and cried, told stories, watched movies, and toasted to Mom and Dad every chance we got! We went to dinner together and, occasionally, with some of Pat's friends.

I met up with an old hospice friend, Barbara, who lived in the Charleston area. Gia took us on a tour of Charleston and the surrounding areas. We celebrated Easter at her home. We were together and making new family memories. We needed that time to grieve and hold each other. Our parents gathered us for all celebrations. Everything centered around them, and now it was up to us.

Mom and Dad had the most beautiful funeral service. Family and friends joined for Mass with specially chosen music, military honors at the gravesite, and a deluxe reception with Jooj's picture boards and place settings. Flowers adorned the room, while friends and family freely mingled in heartfelt embraces. A memorial program with pictures by Pat and a special holy card by me was given to every-one. Nothing was too much for this couple. "That's Amore" was sung one more time in their honor. We gave them over to the God who created them. And we walked proudly into the future with their love and guidance leading us.

Epilogue

I recently celebrated my 78th birthday. And going back over all that I shared with you, I should be right up there with Methuselah, who the Bible says lived 1,418 years! I can scarcely believe I've made it this far. However, after writing this book, it has become more real to me how blessed I've been.

Dad said, "Write it down."

My friends have said, "Write it down."

So, I wrote it down! And it's all true!

Holidays are not the same. My sisters and I have our own commitments, and we live too far apart, which makes gathering difficult. We FaceTime every month or for special occasions. We are trying to be deliberate in planning our get-together. Mom and Dad showed us what family was all about. We will do it. We are Hermanitas, forever!

So, what's on the horizon for me now? Well, I just might pick up my guitar and get those calluses back. I am an art major, after all, so perhaps I have some portraits to finish. I've had my brother's pictures on the easel for years.

There is a new addition to our home. After Mom and Dad passed, the emptiness was deafening. So, we got a dog. Actually, he got us! Our neighbor's dogs had a litter of 10 pedigree yellow labs. We got number seven.

His name is Jake. He fills our lives and our hearts with so much love. He is a year and a half old now and will probably outlive us. I love him with my whole heart. He has a bit too much energy for this old gal, but hey, I've dealt with a lot over these Spirit-led years. Jake is the "Amen" to it all!

Peace and all good to you, my friends,

Rosie

My love forever!

About the Author
+ Contact Info

Rosalie G. Robles

"Trust in God's guidance."

This is the philosophy by which Rosalie G. Robles has lived. With more than five decades of professional experience in ministry, Ms. Robles is a recognized figure in spiritual and religious guidance. She lends her services as Chaplain to Skagit Hospice Services, LLC, specializing in Spiritual Direction. Ms. Robles also provides ministry for all occasions, including weddings, baptisms, and funerals.

She is a motivational speaker and author of *Football Doesn't Have to be a Dirty Word: A Woman's Guide to Understanding the Sport.*

Ms. Robles sat with Cambridge Publishing in an interview in which she described her career as driven by a "desire to help individuals during important moments of their lives."

Inspired by her parents, who instilled in her the true meaning of unconditional love, Ms. Robles earned a Bachelor of Arts degree in Art and Education and a Master of Theology in Religious Studies. She served in faith as a Catholic Sister for 35 years, during which time she taught elementary and secondary school, acted as a retreat director, and rendered pastoral ministry.

Today, she is certified through The Federation of Christian Ministries, a proud member of the National Hospice and Palliative Care Organization, and served on the Internal Review Board of Skagit Valley Hospital. She credits her professional success to her parents, the Sisters of St. Joseph of Carondelet, Archbishop Raymond Hunthausen, and Sister Carol Baetz, SM. In 2009, she was chosen as Cambridge Publishing's VIP member of the year.

Ms. Robles currently resides in Mt. Vernon, Washington, with her husband, Ronald Allen. Her extended family includes five stepchildren and seventeen grandchildren. In her spare time, Ms. Robles enjoys playing her guitar, portrait drawing, walking, reading, watching movies, and dining out.

Rosalie G. Robles Christian Ministries provides spiritual services for all events, including weddings, baptisms, and funerals, as well as guidance and counseling.

Ms. Robles can be reached at
RosieRobles84@gmail.com.